The Star in the Sycamore

Donna—
Thanks for
keeping Kalamazoo
Green!

Best, Tom Springer

Published by Mission Point Press
2554 Chandler Rd.
Traverse City, MI 49696
(231) 421-9513
www.MissionPointPress.com

ISBN: 978-1-950659-65-4
Library of Congress Control Number: 2020907462

Printed in the United States of America

The
Star
in the
Sycamore

*Discovering Nature's
Hidden Virtues in the
Wild Nearby*

Tom
Springer

Mission Point Press

CONTENTS

Introduction:
Wherever the Hawks
May Find You

For a Midwest writer, winter is by far the best writing season. There are no rivers to fish, no lawn to mow, no garden to hoe. Outside, the earth's rimy crust may be as hard and drear as the moons of Saturn. Yet inside, by the motherly warmth of a fire, a crop of good words can sprout like spring lettuce in a hoop house. Except that wasn't the case during a winter four years ago. I'd lost motivation and inspiration (though not procrastination — I had plenty of that) and the words just wouldn't flow.

The cures for writer's block usually involve scribbling/ typing like mad until something readable takes form on a page. But until now, I'd never heard of a remedy that involved this: a series of mystic encounters with large birds that eat raw meat for a living.

The first visitation came in early February, on my morning commute to Battle Creek. There, perched in a dead elm north of Athens on M-66, was a red-tailed hawk: proud, fierce and vigilant as only a bird of prey can be. He must've been ready for some plundering motorist to serve up a ration of morning roadkill on his asphalt buffet line. It entranced me enough that I slowed down for a closer look, which proved startling in the extreme. As our eyes met, I swear that a jolt of hawkish voltage flashed between us. He didn't as much look at me as *through* me.

From then on, the hawk fellowship must've spread the word that this was a man who bore watching. I began to see hawks in places and in numbers I'd never encountered before. By rivers, near bridges, along highways and rooftops. The next to the last of these was boldly intrusive. With casual majesty, he soared a mere five feet from my office window. Twenty-two years in that building — with way too much of it spent staring out windows — and I'd never seen anything like it.

Yet it was a hawk that appeared during my lunchtime walk along the Battle Creek River that finally kicked my tail feathers into gear.

I was lost in thought at the time, my head foggy from a morning of meetings. Then, fast on the wings of fate, my deliverance came. From some unseen aerie of cloud, a red-tail whooshed past my ear and snatched a starling in mid-flight. For a few seconds, their struggle was nature-documentary epic. They rolled and caromed on the walking path in full-feathered combat. But the red-tail's cruel talons made short work of it. The hapless starling soon lay warm and limp for the picking.

Bad news for the starling, yes — but not so for me. It was a true bolt from the blue; an encounter with "the wild nearby" no less transcendental than if I'd spent 30 minutes perched above a Grand Canyon talus slope.

The fact that I'd even stopped to watch was an act of leisure uncommon for a mid-day power walker. Take time to gaze on the peaceable river and green arch of trees overhead? Nope! Have to move fast and get the maximum aerobic benefit. Use this outdoor respite for some creative daydreams? Nope! Have to fret, nonstop, over vexing people and big projects lined up two miles away in a stuffy office.

But on this day, a keen-eyed raptor had rescued me from the bit and bridle of daily routine. What an unexpected pleasure to watch this ancient drama play out. To witness such aerial poetry in the weedy margins of a city best known for a cereal-box tiger and his frosted flakes of corn. In a lifetime of lunch breaks, I'd never seen anything like it.

How could any writer, even one fallen away, witness such a spectacle and not write about it? Short of pecking out the story with his beak, there's not much more the hawk could do by way of inspiration. Back at my desk, where I'm not supposed to write personal stories on company time, I couldn't help but break the rules. The words spilled out clean and well-ordered, as they do when there's something worthy to write about.

It wasn't much, just six or seven tight paragraphs that I had no plans to publish. But the long-absent vigor and purpose were there, all fueled by the hawk's primal energy and spirit. Once you've lost that writerly feeling it's immeasurably good to have it return. I got on a roll after that and wrote a string of essays in the year that followed.

As much as anything, this book is about those rare times when a ray of the luminous penetrates the foggy ground clutter of everyday life. These are mountain top experiences, absent the mountains. I've found them in the crook of a broken tree on a starry night; in a divine mess of fish caught from a little river gone wild in the city. Such encounters are especially life-giving for those of us compelled to work indoors. They ground us in the feral power of creation, an antidote to the stale office air in our nostrils and synthetic carpet squares under our feet.

To showcase these moments, I've divided this book into seven seasons. They may seem arbitrary, but I find them no less precise than the calendar-bound rigidity of spring, summer, fall and winter. Does anyone *really* believe that summer begins on June 21? No, the first ripe Michigan strawberries say summer to me, just as a sumac that flames crimson in an August fencerow sends up the first semaphore flag of autumn. For others, the seasons may turn with the first whiff of lilacs or last basket of tomatoes rescued from the garden before a killing frost. While these milestones aren't measured by celestial reckoning, they are no less a mini-solstice unto themselves. Learning to observe and honor them can greatly enrich a life.

Now as for the hawks, my friend Roger Taylor from Kalamazoo, who hosts a weekly bird show on WKZO-AM radio, doesn't see raptors in the same exalted light that I do. "Sure, they're big and strong," he says, "but they're not very bright." Basically, he views birds of prey as avian gym rats: sharp eyes, big beaks, nasty talons, but not much brains behind the hardware. Fair enough, Roger. Except that the ones I've seen have certainly impressed the hell out of me.

Nevertheless, some questions remain. Once the wild nearby has our number, will it reveal other miracles that were heretofore overlooked? Will there be instructive visits from river turtles, forgotten stars and sentient sycamores? And for now, did all these red-tails really do this for my benefit? Or could it be, as my wonderfully logical wife says, that "there's just more hawks now than there used to be?" Time will tell. But I hope the hawks will, too.

FIRST ICE TO WINTER'S
LONG LAMENT

The Remembered Mercy
of Broken Things

Bret's ½-ton pickup, tastefully dented and rusted per farm truck specifications, backed into our barn driveway on a winter Saturday with a special delivery. Attached to the rear hitch was an empty flatbed trailer that was long enough to carry another truck if necessary.

"That's a pretty big rig just to haul 50 pounds of frozen meat in," I hollered, over the phlegmy cough of the pickup's exhaust.

"It would be," Bret said, "if this was my only stop. But I'm headed to Muncie (Indiana) for a load of hay after this. I found it on Craigslist. There's none around here because of the drought. They want $100 for a round bale if you can believe it."

It was a custom delivery from Bret and Debbie Green's M&M Beefalo Farm in nearby Mendon, Michigan. The packages we unloaded were frozen so hard that they clanked like porcelain plates when we stacked them in the freezer.

A beefalo is two-thirds cattle and one-third buffalo. It's leaner than cattle, but with a wilder, more complex flavor. Bret feeds his animals hay, pasture grass, green corn stalks, some grain and even over-ripe watermelons when he can get them. But no growth hormones. They live an agreeable, outdoor life, until, as farmer/writer Joel Salatin writes, "they have one bad day at the end of it."

"I hope *this* batch lasts you!" said Bret with a conspiratorial grin.

We usually buy a quarter of a beefalo from him each fall, but this year we needed a second order. That's because misfortune intervened — although that was a secret known only to me, my wife, a few family members, and now, our cattleman.

The misfortune befell us on a Saturday evening in July, one of those lingering, saffron-twilight interludes that's perfect for grilling burgers over hardwood coals in the backyard. As I fiddled with stick matches and kindling to start the fire, I asked Emily to retrieve two packages of 1/3-pound patties from the freezer in the barn. Surely a nine-year-old could handle that.

"Be sure to shut the freezer door *tight!*" I instructed. I said it in a shrill, fatherly tone, born of the time-tested expectation that such dictates often fall on deaf ears.

Seconds later, Emily sailed passed with packages in hand, ran them to the house and within a minute was back outside on her trampoline.

After a quick defrost in the microwave, the meat was soon asizzle on the wood-fired grill. It's an imprecise operation. There's no control knob on an open fire, no steel burners to ensure an even distribution of heat and flame. You're forever flipping here and nudging there to center the meat between the too-hot spots and the too-cold spots. You know the patties are ready when the muddy brown "done" juice seeps out and dangles from the grill's underside like a high-protein stalactite.

Campfire cooking in mid-summer makes for a lot of sweating and squatting, but the imprimatur from my eldest daughter, Abby, made it all worthwhile.

"Dad," her picky eminence pronounced, "these are the *best* burgers."

And so they are. Beefalo patties, even when cooked well-done as my wife insists hers be, retain a ruddy color and rich flavor. Garnish them with pickles, garden lettuce and home-grown tomatoes and you've got a prize dish that would fetch $15 at an artisanal burger joint.

But I didn't realize until the next afternoon that this would be our last beefalo cookout of the season. As I was mowing by the barn, an ominous thought came to mind: "Had I checked the freezer door last night?"

It's an old freezer with a weak door seal that must be *firmly* closed. Along with writing *firmly* in italics now, I had used my *italicized voice* to warn my daughter about the finicky ways of old appliances. (Further proof that italics, whether written or spoken, are the last refuge of anemic writers and ineffective parents.)

From 30 feet away, I could see that the door *had not been* firmly closed. It had, in fact, been left ajar … for 24 hours. And, the barn's indoor thermometer now read 92 degrees! I instinctively shut the freezer door *firmly*, as if doing that now made a whit of difference. Then I re-opened it slowly, with the wincing trepidation usually reserved for one who has, with a sickening crunch, just backed over a child's favorite toy in the driveway.

"Son of a, son of a, son of a … arrgggghhh!"

It wasn't just the packages of beefalo — about 25 pounds — that were thawed and dripping a wretched pink fluid onto the floor. There were also five pounds of gorgeous steelhead and Chinook salmon filets, caught from a boat on Lake Michigan. We'd won the trip in a church raffle and it would not be repeated. There were 20 bags of strawberries, picked on my wife's family farm, the promise of winter fruit smoothies to come (and now bound for the compost heap). There were venison steaks for which I'd traded six pounds of honey from our beehives.

It was such a wasted blessing. In all, several hundred dollars' worth of food had been reduced to an oozing heap of vacuum-sealed offal. Apart from the money, these were prized provisions of a sort that only our home place can provide. We'd caught the fish, picked the berries and harvested the honey that we'd used for barter. It was our hands and those of our friends that had done this: Bret and Debbie, Brian and John. Their care and handiwork were the food's provenance.

The loss was beyond infuriating. Someone — I knew exactly who — would have to pay for it. Picture a hot, dirty, angry father as he stomps to the house. Imagine his fury about to be unleashed, channeled into a firm tongue-lashing about waste and carelessness that a guilty child would not soon forget. But as I neared the patio, and the magma of recrimination reached eruption point, a long-forgotten memory leaped up and assailed me.

It was of a 10-year-old boy on a playground outside the Catholic school in Three Rivers, where he'd come for Saturday morning catechism class. It was December, and a big gray puddle had frozen there to form an impromptu ice rink. It was a perfect place to whoop and slide with friends before someone's Mom, with a beehive hairdo, drilled her charges on the Holy Trinity.

The boy had gotten his first pair of eyeglasses earlier that week, and what a marvelous gift they had been. For the first time ever, he could see in fine detail the high branches of tall maples that lined the street. I must surely protect such an expensive accoutrement, thought the boy. So, with reasoning that would soon prove recklessly imbecilic, he removed the glasses ... and tucked them in his *back pocket*. It was, inevitably, just moments before the clumsy, giraffe-legged boy fell back first onto the ice. The new glasses shattered, and thus did their fragments dig painfully into his skinny buttocks.

My father was a barber, and those new glasses of mine

must've him cost a day's worth of haircuts. On the way home, I feared his wrath. But it's telling that my last memory of the event ends here. All I recall is that he didn't explode. He lashed me neither with his hands nor his tongue. Did he sigh deeply and wonder how such an addlebrained son could have sprung from his loins? Perhaps. Yet he never let on that he did. And because he didn't, then neither could I vent my fatherly wrath on a daughter who was too young to master the ways of a jinky freezer.

I'm not sure why my freezer had to break before this decades-old lesson from my father bore fruit. But I do know that modern technology usually insulates us from such natural consequences. Since we can eat frozen venison in July, and fresh Chilean grapes in January, the seasonal wisdom of our ancestors can seem irrelevant. Quaint, even. So, when Bret blamed "the drought" on his December hay shortage, I was surprised. The drought? From last summer? That was old news for me and anyone else who doesn't farm.

But when Bret says the "drought" he doesn't qualify it with "last summer's drought." It's still in the present tense for him. It's as real as a barn full of bawling beefalo that need hay from somewhere if they're to survive the winter. Bret must bear the drought's burdens until spring rains make his dormant pastures green again.

I told this to Nancy, who worked fall weekends at her family's orchard, and she understood completely. The previous March, weeks of record high temperatures in the 80s had made the fruit trees blossom early. Inevitably, when the weather corrected to seasonal norms, frosts came and destroyed nearly all the apple blossoms. Without blossoms there's no fruit and the trees won't bloom again until the next year.

But by fall? When customers came for their squash, pumpkins, garlands of onions, ears of dried Indian corn and, oh yes, bags of apples?

"We're sorry," Nance would say, "but there's hardly any due to the hard frost last spring. We hope they'll bounce back next year."

Some customers were puzzled, others a bit put off.

"Well, yes," they seemed to insinuate, "but we want our apples *now*."

As if, through some digital chicanery, we could subvert natural law and produce pixelated Ida Reds on a virtual assembly line. Thankfully, we can't. Yet next season, given the trees' stored-up root energy, there could well be a bumper apple crop. While last spring may be long forgotten — at least by humans — we can count on nature to keep an accurate ledger.

For a tree, the ledger of fat and lean years is easily visible to the naked eye. And not just in the annual crop of fruit, acorns or seedpods they produce. Trees inscribe their cellulosic history within the growth rings of every branch and trunk. As a boy, I used to wonder why people couldn't be more like that. Wouldn't it be crazy fun to lop off an arm or finger and count the rings? (To a curious boy, such thoughts are not morbid.) While not anatomically true, I may have been on to something. People and trees alike do bear within their circumference a lived history of physical and spiritual growth, along with scars of injury and hardship.

In the poem "Rings," Joseph Bruchac conveyed that sentiment about a load of old-growth trees he saw chained to an Oregon logging truck. It pained him to see their sacred stories laid bare in the naked annuities of severed trunks. Even the smallest log, Bruchac observed:

> *Has more than a hundred*
> *scars around*
> *the wrists of seasons.*

Alexander Pope, writing in 1732, had younger trees in mind (and certainly curious boys) when he composed this proverb: "Just as the twig is bent so the tree's inclined." The trick here, with trees and humans, is to bend with judicious care. When maple saplings are bound too tight in the upright position, the guy wires that are meant to stabilize them can leave wounds of their own. They can even girdle a tree and kill it. To prevent that, one must loosen the wires as needed to accommodate new growth. It's an apt reminder that all discipline should lead to freedom, not enslavement.

An image closer to home comes from Rachel Peden (1901-1975), an essayist and Indiana farm wife who wrote of rural life with a luminous sense of the ordinary. While raking her front yard, she compares the tree's annual crop of leaves — meticulously grown from bud to leaf, then recklessly discarded as debris — with her own endless round of meals cooked, beds made, chickens fed and floors swept.

But the colored leaves now lying on the grass are not all. Inside the dark, rough trunk, the tree has added a new layer of live wood around its core … And something remains from a year of farm living, too … a layer of strength that will persist as a permanent record, long after the tedious household chores are raked up and carried out to the midden to disintegrate.

Peden strikes me as one who would've understood the remembered mercy of broken things. A traditional farm is a place abundant with life and death, wonder and catastrophe. There are times when even the strong can't bear to hear the undiluted truth of it all — much less a girl who dresses up her cat in purple doll pajamas. But Emily will hear about the freezer disaster someday, I can promise that. Revenge may be a dish best-served cold, but parental-induced guilt is an entrée that's always in season.

The Christmas Tree
You Don't Know Beans About

Each year, with the coming of Advent, I become like a Hebrew prophet of antiquity who can his hold tongue no longer. For within me doth burn a great truth that I must reveal to believer and unbeliever alike. It involves an oft-repeated detail of Christian history that we in the West only half understand. Specifically, the eating habits of one John the Baptist.

John's earthly mission, should it bear repeating, was to proclaim the coming of a Messiah who turned out to be his cousin, Jesus of Nazareth. John called for widespread repentance and baptized his followers, including Jesus himself, in the Jordan River. John's travels often took him into the rocky hills and badlands of the Judean Desert, now part of Israel. It was ideal terrain for a self-styled preacher and ascetic who often locked horns with civil and religious authorities. By all accounts, John was a woolly and unvarnished character.

In this Gospel passage, read on the second Sunday in Advent, John comes across as semi-feral:

"John wore clothing made of camel's hair and had a leather belt around his waist. His food was locusts and wild honey." (Matthew, 3:4)

While John's hirsute wardrobe sounds plausible enough, it's the reference to eating locusts that remains problematic. When I first heard this verse as a kid growing up Catholic in Florida, I couldn't imagine anything more revolting. We had eastern lubber grasshoppers down there (*Romalea microptera*). They were black, yellow and red; horrid things, some four inches long, that clung with monstrous intent to the window screens. And to hear my catechism teacher tell it, John the Baptist would dunk these things in honey for breakfast? That disturbed me more than the hairy legged nun who I once saw order a *plain* MacDonald's hamburger (no ketchup, mustard, onions or pickle). For her, this small act of self-denial was condiment enough.

It wasn't until decades later, while reading "Tree Crops," a classic horticultural work by Joseph Russell Smith, that I found a fuller explanation.

First of all, it's likely that John the Baptist really did eat locusts. They were, in fact, the only insects that met the kosher dietary requirements of Jews, and later, the Halal dietary requirements of Muslims. Locusts were, and still are, a nutritious food source eaten across Africa, Asia and Central America. High in fatty acids and minerals, their dried weight contains up to 62 percent protein. Locusts can be pickled, dried, smoked, boiled, roasted, grilled, stir fried — basically, whatever the cook deems necessary to lessen their colossal ick factor.

Yet for North Americans and Europeans, there's an untold story about locusts that's been overlooked in the Bible's English translation. Namely, that the other locusts John the Baptist ate were likely the seed pods that grow on the locust *tree*. The six-inch pods contain leguminous (bean-like) seeds. Around the Mediterranean basin, the tree goes by many names: locust, carob, carob bean, sugar pod and, drumroll please, St. John's bread *(Ceratonia siliqua)*. Apparently, they've known all along.

The beans inside the locust pods can be dried and roasted to make carob, a caffeine-free chocolate substitute. The next time you eat yogurt, read the label. There's a good chance it includes locust bean gum, a thickener derived from the crushed beans. In arid lands with scant pasture, the high-protein beans have long been an important fodder for livestock.

In times of famine and strife, locust beans can also provide emergency rations for humans. Residents of Malta ate them during World War II, when the besieged island nation became the most bombed place on Earth. And, as we read in the Gospel of Luke, it appears that the Prodigal Son would've happily joined them. In Jesus' telling, the young man in the parable was a half-starved wastrel who hired out as a farm hand after he blew his inheritance on drink and prostitutes: "He longed to fill his stomach with the *pods* (italics mine) that the pigs were eating, but no one gave him anything." (Luke

15-16). As Jesus suggests, someone that hungry would've gladly chowed down on locusts, Paleo-style, sans the honey or lemongrass stir-fry.

Locust trees are also native to North America, although they come from a different botanical family than the Mediterranean kind. In rich Midwestern soils, honey locusts *(Gleditsia triacanthos)* can reach heights of 60-70 feet, as they do in a grove near my home. In summer, their lacy, fern-like foliage casts a shade that's cool, but nicely mottled. The locust's almond-sized leaves can be easily swept and won't clog storm drains. This makes nursery-bred locusts popular as urban street trees.

There's one trait, though, that tame varieties of locusts have had bred out of them: their thorns. And for good reason. For these aren't the tolerable little thorns you'll find on a rose bush or raspberry cane. Oh no. The dastardly, three-inch pig stickers on a wild honey locust feel as stout and sharp as a mini-bayonet. There are three by my writing chair and each time I mess with one (like just now!) I manage to stab myself.

For me, their fierce animosity presents an evolutionary puzzle. Why would a large, graceful tree need such a hostile defense? What's it afraid of? It's got bark as thick as a red oak or sugar maple. Shouldn't that be body armor enough? No resident raccoon, possum or even bear could cause a honey locust much harm. One argument I've heard is that locust thorns once served as protection against giant tree sloths, saber-toothed cats and other toothsome, long-clawed beasts that disappeared after the Ice Age 12,000 years ago.

Perhaps locusts will eventually get the memo and morph into something less prickly. Until then, their over-the-top nasty thorns seem more offensive than defensive; more for gratuitous harm, in the way of fallen humanity, than for natural resistance. In this respect, they pose a question as much theological as biological: Could it be that even trees need a process of rebirth to perfect what evolution began? When St. Paul talks about "all creation groaning as in the pains of childbirth" as it awaits redemption (Romans 8:22), it does sound like the misanthropic locust fits the bill.

For now, I'm content with the seed pods we collected on our walk. They'll winter in the barn and, come spring, should sprout into seedlings that will serve as an Alpha to Omega remembrance. Their brown, leathery pods will recall the wilderness sojourn of John, who foretold the coming of a carpenter-king born to serve the poor and the oppressed. Their lacy foliage will remind me of Palm Sunday hosannas, and the fickle nature of public acclaim that turned murderous by Good Friday afternoon. While there are other trees in that story — the accursed fig, the sycamore where little Zacchaeus perched — it's the thorny crown and lifegiving bread of a locust that may embody it best. It's a rare symbol of Advent and Easter as one.

15

As Dusk Falls
in a Pileated Land

Late-afternoon on Christmas Eve Day, and finally, a spare hour to recollect before the holiday. And to clear the head, what better than a long walk in the country away from everything that jingles or bears a price tag?

At least that should've been the case. But you know how we mortals are: It's the everyday gifts we most overlook, and the routine of this three-mile walk was one of them. Such over-familiarity is a pitfall of the rooted life. After 20-plus years on the same route you, too, could describe it blindfolded. You'd know which neighbor's house to covet and which cobbled-up barn to pass judgment on. You'd know which untied dogs mean business and which ones will merely yip their fool heads off. So, on I trudged, lamenting how often our life can drone along on autopilot, our days and even holidays a mobius loop of rote predictability. Such are the first-world problems of a healthy and well-fed man, lost in a lethargy of his own making.

The leaden skies certainly didn't help. In southern Michigan, a pewter dome of gloom can descend for weeks on end during early winter. It's then, during the shortest days, that we need a magic thread to lead us from the labyrinth of December's darkness. Or failing that, a minor deity sent by the Powers of the Air to banish the doldrums.

The first of these was unexpected — and otherwise insignificant. Anywhere else, it's just another little bird. But the clouds were solstice gray; the hickories and white oaks all gunmetal and monochrome; my own breath a mist of dull silver as I sloshed through the roadside slush. It was then that a red comet shot across the road with all the visual punch — *Zip! Kapow! Whammo!* — of a comic book epithet. It was a male cardinal, maybe two ounces max, give or take a few sunflower seeds. Yet nothing else in that somnolent landscape could've been as bright. He wasn't so much a bird as a crimson exclamation point; an antidote to everything hackneyed and over-wrought about the season. I was, in the words of C.S. Lewis, "surprised by joy."

A wakeup call like that can't help but jar open the doors of perception. I've waded and fished enough Michigan rivers to know how one natural discovery can presage another. On a July evening, after a bass leaps to snatch the night's first mayfly, your reptilian brain kicks into overdrive. You see in the dusk with new clarity, hyper alert for a big hatch that will sweep up the river on gossamer wings and incite the fish to a feeding frenzy. You see, too, other creatures once overlooked. The turkeys at roost in a high sycamore overhead. A mink, usually sleek and secretive, now revealed in a vined tangle of riverbank.

True to form, the next deity showed up about three minutes later. And by comparison, the cardinal was only a warm-up act. This second bird was colossally larger, 18-20 inches from beak to tail. It was lanky and angular, a mini-pterodactyl that could've flown in from the set of a Flintstones movie. Its black-and-white striped face was set below a brilliant red crest, like one of those gloriously anti-social punk mohawks of 1970s' London vintage. Add a two-foot wingspan to the picture and there you have it: the pileated woodpecker, the largest bird of its kind in North America. Moments later his Lordship flapped off (a pileated does not flit) into a silver maple swamp by the road. As he flew, the undersides of his wings flashed downy white through the woods. This was the first pileated I'd seen in my corner of Michigan.

I sidestepped an empty quart bottle of Bud Light and eased into the tall timber for a closer look. A host of birds had sought shelter there from the harsh north wind. Downy woodpeckers and nuthatches chittered among the branches and pecked daintily at the trunks. Not so the pileated. He'd cock his head back at a 45-degree angle, then beak-slam forward with a *thunk-thunk-thunk* that rang out like Thor's own hammer. The neat pile of uniform chips he left behind could've been made by a skilled carpenter with a wood chisel.

The big bird's trademark call was just as outlandish as his plumage. Reportedly, the pileated's staccato voice led Walter Lantz to create his Woody the Woodpecker cartoon charac-

ter in the 1940s. To hear the half-mad "nuk-nuk-nuk-nuk-nuk"
echo through the woods at dusk makes that sound plausible.
I listened to the avian stand-up routine until my cold feet could
take no more. It was one of the rare times when I wished I had
a camera to capture the moment.

To spot a pileated near my home was a marvel. Yet the fact
that I found it here wasn't entirely unexpected. Anyone who
seeks solace in the outdoors will eventually find a stretch of
beach, mountain, desert, forest or little woods that attracts
them like nowhere else. We find deep contentment there,
buoyed by consolations that spring from sources unknown.
At times, it can seem that only a thin, corporeal membrane
separates such places from heaven and earth.

For me, the anointed geography includes this flat stretch of
country road almost smack dab on the 42nd parallel. Why?
Well, once you've been grounded somewhere by fate, choice
and inertia, I suppose inspiration must find you where it will.
I do know that I've seen and heard the mundane speak in
tongues here. That they have done so as a dead coyote, phantom cougar or locust tree with hideous thorns makes them no
less momentous. As for the cardinal and pileated, I can only
guess that they showed up to teach me anew about gratitude.

Then again, maybe my mind simply made a connection
between the two birds as a coping strategy to escape holiday
overload. I am happy to profit from both explanations.

But it was Christmas Eve and the gentle yoke of family obligations awaited at home. And what I found waiting there were
two eminently useful gifts: a warmer pair of walking shoes

and a new camera, the traditional kind that isn't built into a cell phone. What's more, in the prescient ways of nature, I'd also been given two red-crested reasons for using them both.

A New Year in the Garden
of Good and Weevil

Of all the in-between seasons, the January thaw can be the most tantalizing. For a few rapturous days the thaw looks backward and forward like the month's namesake god, the two-faced Janus. It feels part Indian summer and part early spring, with temperatures that run 10 or 15 degrees above normal. It tempts us to believe, against all meteorological evidence to the contrary, that winter just might end two months early this year.

Then, inevitably, the thaw pulls the football away in mid-kick, and we're tricked once more by its fool's gold promises. The north wind returns with an icy vengeance, and we're left with nothing of holiday cheer but a half-eaten cheeseball in the fridge.

Still, as much as any resolution, the thaw does present us with an existential choice for the New Year ahead. We can ignore the balmy sunshine and grumble about "paying for all this later," or we can live in the present and freely imbibe of the thaw's fleeting pleasures.

Personally, I'd rather raise a cup of cheap happy to the latter. I learned that three years ago when the January thaw jumped the gun and showed up on Dec. 31. At 8 a.m. on New Year's Day, the kitchen window thermometer read 42 degrees — and would climb to a sunny 53 by day's end. Most spring-like of all was the wind: fresh, bright and alive with the unsullied promise of a new year. It drove away the winter doldrums, not to mention the scrum line of minor litter (school papers, junk mail, junk food wrappers) that emanated from the driveway parking space.

Not far away sits our 600 square-foot vegetable garden. From early May to mid-September, it's a touchstone of daily existence. Over a season, I can spend a month of afternoons there. It's a grocery store, gymnasium, agricultural college and prayer labyrinth rolled into one. After the thaw, when I went to retrieve some driveway trash from the garden, my eye was drawn to an oasis strip of green. It wasn't a complete surprise. I'd planted a row of turnips and carrot seeds in late August and planned to dig them by Thanksgiving. Once it turned too cold and snowy in December, I lost interest. Since the turnips hadn't been covered with leaf mulch, I figured they'd be frozen to mush by now.

But that wasn't the case at all. With the snow melted, the submerged turnips pulled easily from the soft soil. And what a cheery sight they were. Fist-sized globes of round, shiny flesh; purple on top, with undersides as pure white as a new baseball. As a root crop, it took me awhile to overcome the turnip's Russian-babushka-with-chin-whiskers reputation. Now, I scarcely go a week without eating one. They're a zesty substitute for potatoes when diced for soups. They make great "carrot sticks" when sliced lengthwise and eaten plain or dipped in hummus.

As for the carrots, they were still babies: three inches long, not much bigger around than a fat pencil. But these weren't the bogus "baby" carrots sold in stores. No, those are simply big, tasteless clunkers that some machine has whittled down to finger size. These little beauties were sweet, crisp, tangy — a delicacy almost too pretty to eat. Almost.

When the balmy south wind died down around 5 p.m., there was just enough time for a late afternoon walk. And, one last incantation of January thaw mojo before a cold front moved in the next day. Halfway down the road, I saw an onion along the shoulder where a snowbank had been. Then another and another until I realized that they weren't onions. They were flower bulbs. Dozens and dozens of them. Gladiolus, to be precise. I stuffed them in my jacket pockets until I looked like a squirrel with his cheeks full of acorns.

It's a mystery that's easily enough explained. There's a farm nearby that grows and sells mail-order gladiolus bulbs and tends a 60-acre field south of here. Come July, a gorgeous pastel tide of salmon, lavender and raging pink stretches to the horizon. Then for two weeks in October, a convoy of tractors and farm wagons heaped with harvested bulbs rumbles past. Enough must have jostled off to turn my walk into a cheapskate's treasure hunt.

On the next Sunday, we celebrated the Feast of Epiphany. It's an old Greek word that means manifestation — as in, when gods and goddesses made their fearful presence known to mortals. Of course, it's *presents* we know Epiphany for today, in remembrance of those brought by three Iranian astrologers to Bethlehem. While the Christmas season once began on Dec. 25, it now ends there (otherwise known as the Feast of the Fourth Quarter Retail Bonanza). The party's long over by the time the seers and their dusty camels arrive on Jan. 6. Epiphany doesn't even rate its own college bowl game.

During the Epiphany sermon, (sorry, Padre) my mind wandered back to my unexpected presents from the day before. The carrots, little flowers to be enjoyed at once, orange slivers of instant delight. Their vitamins help us see better in the long, dark nights ahead. The turnips, honest and enduring, that could last until spring in a root cellar or unheated storeroom. Their purple and creamy white faces are in their own way regal and true.

And the gladiolus? Of these gifts, it's the hardest to appreciate. To think that something this small, brown, shriveled and cruddy can entomb in its cells a spectacular flag of summer. The gardening books, of which I have too many, say that gleaned gladiolus bulbs won't survive. They should be dug, dried and stored in a cool place soon after Halloween.

You can't just dump them unprotected along a road in pearls-before-swine fashion.

Or so they say. I've seen a "dead" oak sapling send up a four-foot sucker from its trunk that's stouter and heartier than the tree it replaced. I've watched a plug of big bluestem grass wait three springs before it finally sent up a long blade of green, a chlorophyll hosanna sent to bestir a doubting world. In a similar way, that's what the thaw does: It arrives as a harbinger, however brief, of promised regeneration to come. And as Dana Gioia makes clear in his poem "New Year's," a clean start in January is gift enough:

> *The new year always brings us what we want*
> *Simply by bringing us along — to see*
> *A calendar with every day uncrossed,*
> *A field of snow without a single footprint.*

Requiem for a Contented Man

       The layer-cake loveliness of new snow always looks best when left unmarred by track or trail. But who could resist six fresh inches on the walking paths behind the barn? My chore boots sent up little geysers of white as I chugged past the dried stalks of goldenrod, their raiment long since distilled by our bees into dark honey. Callie, our eight-month-old border collie, kicked up a sugary rooster tail as she slalomed around the withered canes of blackberries and buggy whip trunks of little oaks.

  After a week of sickness, death and grief, the glisten of cold air was good medicine.

  We'd lost my father in the wee hours of Tuesday morning. He, proprietor of the one-man, small town barbershop where he'd stood, clipped, and ministered until age 82, when the tremors of Alzheimer's finally turned his strong hands weak. He, proclaimer of time-worn aphorisms that from his mouth rang no less true: "Plan your work and work your plan ...

Always do a little more than what's expected … If you can't say something nice about somebody, don't say anything at all … If you're waiting on me, you're backing up." (That last one, as with several of his koanlike sayings, we could never quite figure out.)

Yet in the end, he couldn't say anything. A stroke had taken his voice and pneumonia had stolen his very breath. There'd be no last words of the cinematic variety, with the family gathered in unison at bedside.

Absent that, I had tried a week earlier to sum things up for the both of us.

On this particular day, he'd had a restless, trying afternoon and needed to calm down for the night. So, I began to recount touchstone memories we both knew and loved. They're mostly true, but have been greatly honed by retelling, their edges now polished smooth as Petoskey stones on a Lake Michigan beach. The stories were part litany, part lamentation. They brought to mind the Kaddish that a good Jewish son prays after his father's passing. Except that my gentile version had fish and trees in it:

> *"Dad, you remember how sick you got on that crowded Army troop ship headed to Korea? For two weeks you slept on the deck, ate nothing but Hi-Ho crackers and puked off the fantail."*

> *"Dad, you remember the first time you took me fishing? I caught these puny sunfish by the Langley*

Covered Bridge and begged to take them home. You put them in a pail on the back porch, and the next morning I cried because the cats got them and left nothing but guts and bones."

"Dad, you remember how in Florida we'd dip blue crabs and jumbo shrimp off the pier by the Melbourne library? One night I dropped that long-handled net into the water — it still had crabs in it — and you didn't even cuss me out. At least, not much."

"Dad, you remember how me and Jeff dug sand fleas for bait while you waded into the ocean to catch whiting with a bamboo cane pole? And that day when you showed the snowbird with a fancy surf rod how to catch fish?"

"Dad, you remember when I lost that big steelhead in the Muskegon River below the Hardy Dam? We camped that night, and a blizzard half blew our tent down. That was the same storm that sunk the Edmund Fitzgerald."

"Dad, you remember when I called your barber shop from Fort Benning after I earned my Army para-trooper wings? There was no one else in the world that I wanted to tell first."

The priest had earlier given my father last rites, and I left that evening with the sense that I, too, had said my ritual farewell. I was content in that knowledge, as well I should be. For if there was one thing my father knew, lived and radiated, it was contentment.

That is not a virtue we often hear cited in the afterglow of death. People will say that so-and-so loved his family, that he was a good provider or that he liked to build bluebird houses in his garage. But to say he was content? That doesn't sound effusive enough; as platitudes go, it is in fact underwhelming. You'll never see that written on a tombstone, much less a social media post. Who wants to be remembered as someone who just accepted whatever came along? Which is why, when people said this about my father, it made me know that they were telling the truth.

For my Dad, this peace of mind was often expressed in a way that I've found particular to his generation. He whistled while he worked.

"Yeah, we always knew when he was out in the yard," said his longtime neighbor Mark. "I'm not sure *what* he was whistling, but he always sounded so content. It's funny, I was just talking to your brother, and that's the word we both used to describe him: content."

And so he was. My father had a Zen-like ability to derive enjoyment from the commonest elements of life. It certainly helped that he was immune to the guiles of advertising. He was heedless of name brands and the status attached to clothing, cars, restaurants or consumer goods of any kind. By his reckoning, a thing's value was inversely proportional to what he'd paid for it. He would describe his ideal shopping experience as follows:

"I like garage sales where some guy just died who wore clothes in my size."

Among his prized finds was a hideous, salmon-colored linen sports coat. (Obviously, even the deceased hadn't wanted to be caught dead in it.) It was for years a torment to my mother until she re-sold it at a garage sale of her own. And since my thrifty father was cremated, he preserved his wife-approved, blue sport coat for another lucky soul who wears a 44-L.

While no one would ever describe Bill Springer as trendy, he was the first in our family to be cremated. This, of course, eliminates the biological need for a prompt burial. Once the body's natural decay has been forestalled by fire — inert ashes more or less last forever — there's no need to rush. Nevertheless, we stuck to the four- to five-day timetable that's become the American standard for funeral preparation. It is not, as I learned, just a convenient interval dreamed up by the funeral industry. It is instead a wisely ordered interregnum, one attuned to the physical, emotional and spiritual demands that death places on a family.

For us it had the feel of a personal Holy Week. First, the Gethsemane of the deathbed, where he died at 2:35 a.m. with none to share his passing. Then, the cock's crow alarm of the dreaded phone call, followed by a fugue-state drive in darkness to the hospital. Finally, the family's pieta caress of a beloved husband and father — now unburdened of dementia's cross — as his last warmth seeped away.

The next day brought the Arimathean business of burial preparations with the funeral director, a welcome distraction from the carnality of last things. A day later came the visitation, the only time we'll see again such an assemblage of my father's friends and relatives. Next, the Easter promise of the funeral Mass, celebrated by a burly priest in black vestments who must've puffed enough incense smoke from his overheated thurible to cure a shed full of Virginia hams.

As always, the women of our small town held things together. They brought a flood of soups, pies, meats and casseroles; an embarrassment of caloric riches that we thought would never get eaten but did. They sent a flock of sympathy cards, more than 60 at final count, which perched upright on my mother's dining room table like dove wings fixed in repose.

Yet all these gifts and graces don't relieve you from facing the usual ineffable questions. What did the deceased's life really mean? Were they able to solve the peculiar algebra of their existence? What would the world be — for good or ill — if they hadn't been who they were?

A week after my father died, a front-page article in the Three Rivers newspaper gave me a simpler point of comparison. Maybe it was just a straw man, yet the contrast did bring his life into sharper relief. The story dealt with a man who was comptroller for a regional grocery store chain. Their specialty was supermarkets in small towns where larger chain stores won't locate. Given the man's title, he must've earned a generous six-figure salary.

My father also oversaw a valued small-town institution. Generations of kids — such as the funeral director who buried him — had their first haircut in his shop, complete with free lollipop. Although he was "CEO," my Dad never earned an hourly wage, much less a salary. His was all piecework. He didn't make money unless he had clippers in hand and a customer's rear end in the chair. In the last years, as his energy and customers waned, there were days when it scarcely paid to keep the doors open.

The comptroller, as the article explained, loved old American muscle cars. He had *50* of them! Among them were 14 Ford Mustangs, seven Chevrolet Chevelles, five Chevrolet Camaros and four Dodge Challengers.

My Dad enjoyed cars, too, although he never owned a new one. He was partial to used, four-door American sedans, long on legroom, that he'd nurse along into their dotage. He liked to wash them by hand (while whistling, of course) in the front yard. When we lived in Florida, he'd add a cup of kerosene to the rinse bucket which he said kept the ocean spray from rusting the roof. The Depression had taught him to make things last.

The comptroller's job required him to keep certain matters secret; to guard sensitive information that could do harm if made public. To exploit that knowledge would be wrong, and as we shall see, clearly illegal.

The same held true for my father, except that it wasn't profit and earnings statements he was entrusted with. Like Wendell Berry's fictional barber, Jayber Crow, my father's role in the community transcended the prosaic nature of his trade. Cut someone's hair and they'll tell you anything. Cancer scares, marital infidelity, crooked business deals, the gory memories of war. In his role as barber/confessor, it seemed that no human experience was off-limits.

It would've been easier had he been a gossip. Then he could've unloaded his burden over a few beers with his golfing buddies. Instead, on those nights when he was unusually quiet, only my mother knew that he'd heard something bad. When a local crisis or situation would later play out publicly, he'd gently say, "Yeah, I heard about that at the shop but didn't want to say anything."

As for the comptroller, in his regional travels he must've passed through Three Rivers. I don't know if he ever stopped at Bill's Barber Lounge for the best $10 haircut in town. More's the pity if he didn't. Perhaps he could've heard — and profited from — another of my father's favorite axioms: "All things in moderation." The headline to the aforementioned article certainly suggested as much:

Man charged in $6 million Village Market theft

The comptroller, the Michigan Attorney General's office said, had embezzled the $6 million over the course of six years. Small wonder that the popular store in nearby Centreville had to close, a blow from which the village has yet to recover. He'd rigged his company's credit card transfers and used the loot "for his own personal use and enjoyment."

Personal use, yes. But true enjoyment (much less contentment) I doubt. Unless you're Wall Street-mogul rich, can you imagine the nightmare of storage, maintenance and insurance that a fleet of 50 classic cars would require? Add to that the comptroller's sociopathic need to steal ever more money so that he could buy ever more cars. Which he must not have enjoyed very much anyway. If he did, why would he always need to steal more?

No, "personal enjoyment" was my Dad on his front porch on a summer evening with a box of pet treats that made his house a tail-wagging, leash-pulling stop for every dog walker in First Ward. Personal enjoyment was my Dad blissful in his creaky lawn chair beside a campfire with a cold, domestic (read cheap) beer in his hand. Personal enjoyment was my Dad at 5:30 a.m. on Sunday morning in the church basement, where he'd volunteer with his sons to make homemade doughnuts.

There, we let him run the deep fryer until, at age 81 — and this, the only miracle I may ever see — he slipped and stuck three fingers into the bubbling grease … at 400 degrees. We watched aghast as he pulled them out, pink and shiny yet inexplicably unscathed. He gave us a sheepish smile and never said a word about it. I believe that an honorable man, the kind who will pack a sack of bologna and cucumber sandwiches, and take a nervous, 9-year-old boy to dig sassafras roots on a Saturday afternoon, deserves a break like that.

On the day after my Dad's burial I replayed these stories over and over as I walked the trail labyrinth behind our home. Even there was life and death. The black dog tore past like a stroke of Chinese calligraphy across the white parchment of winter. By the barn, gray tufts of rabbit fur and wing swipes on the snow marked where an owl or hawk had swooped in for the kill. Then, from across the field, love personified.

"Tom-m-m-m," a womanly voice called, "dinner's ready!"

Inside, a steaming dish of Nancy's spinach tortellini, rich with home-canned tomatoes, awaited. Ready to eat. Famished. My contentment delayed. Dammit, where are the girls?

It was then, for the first time since his death, that I heard my father speak — except it was in my voice and not his own. "Get down here, or we'll start without you!" I yelled up the stairs. "And if you're waiting on me … well, if you're waiting on me, you're backing up!"

The Grist
of a Handmade Afternoon

Last fall, somewhere on the Great Plains, a clanking combine sliced through a row of sun-cured wheat. From there the golden yield rumbled along the roads of commerce, making stops at a grain elevator, flour mill and grocery store along the way. And now it's come to this: a powdery dust of white on the hands of a girl who's making her first loaf of bread.

"But why do we have to learn to *make* bread?" Emily had asked earlier. "We get all our bread from the store."

We do indeed, which is exactly why we arranged a Sunday afternoon trip to our friend Mary's kitchen. In all my 50-some years, I've never made bread. But there's no reason why my children should be thus deprived. Mom, Dad and the two girls have come to learn what the staff of life smells, feels and tastes like before the plastic wrapper goes on.

The loaves of oatmeal and cinnamon bread take shape on Mary's kitchen counter, now sprinkled deep with wintry drifts of flour. I'd like to help, but it's an old house with a small kitchen, so I adjourn with Mary's husband, Zolton, to his garage woodshop. Here, too, a fine layer of fragrant dust covers everything. Except that it's native hardwoods — cherry, maple and walnut — that perfume the air. Mary and Zolton are creative minimalists and their workspaces reflect that. Like a ship's galley, every square foot of the kitchen and former one-car garage turned workshop has been put to orderly use. The layout befits two artisans disciplined in their craft (Mary's also a writer), with deep roots in the academic village of leafy, hilly streets that adjoin Kalamazoo College. Picture a medieval guild, but with flush toilets and tenure.

The heat's off in Zolton's workshop. Our breath steams in the soft winter light from the big windows as he explains the ways of saws, planers and joiners. On shelves above and around us, he stacks new and used lumber for the chairs, tables and bookcases yet to come. Given Zolton's exacting eye — he's also an architectural photographer — I'd guess that each piece has been hand-chosen for its straight grain and form. None of the warped, knotty, picked-over seconds you'll find in spades at a big-box lumber yard for him.

Still, an unheated workshop in January is no place for prolonged conversation. Besides, what mortal male can resist the allure of fresh-baked anything? We repair inside to savor warm, thick slices perfected by butter and homemade jam.

The latter came from the urban red raspberry patch that Zolton tends outside his south-facing workshop windows.

Then we tell — what else? — bread stories.

"When I was a kid in East Lansing, all we had was Wonder Bread," says Zolton, with a grimace. "But it did make great bait. We'd roll it into little dough balls and fish for carp in the Red Cedar River."

Exactly. Such is our shared, cultural memory of store-bought American bread: a nutritional cipher, without taste or texture — a soulless void consigned to the delivery of boring bologna or the ubiquitous PBJ. It had no identity or purpose of its own, other than to clasp the fixings of our midday blandwich.

"My first taste of *real* bread," I recalled, "was Germany, 1984. We'd been out for two weeks on Army maneuvers and were sick to death of field rations. So, a guy from my recon patrol snuck into town and brought back some loaves of fresh-baked rye. We'd found this old abandoned chapel in the woods, and we ate on the floor as moonlight streamed in through the broken windows. I never knew plain bread could taste so good: great texture, a nutty, yeasty flavor. Then we washed it down with some liter bottles of local Pilsner. Man, that's still one of the best meals I've had anywhere."

After ample servings of reminiscence, there's time for one last stop in the woodshop. On his lathe, Zolton turns out two spinning tops for the girls. Rosy shavings of black cherry (they even smell like cherries) adorn his sweatshirt. The tops are elegant simplicity defined. When spun on a table, they rotate with clean symmetry. For 45 seconds, nary a wobble do they make.

In a world gone mad for efficiency and profit, it can seem pointless and anachronistic to make common things by hand. That's what toy stores and bread machines are for (there's one of the latter rusting in my kitchen closet). But before we use a labor-saving device, maybe we should ask this question: "What better thing will we do with the time we've saved?"

Nothing, as far I can tell. From the raw ingredients of wood, wheat and friendship, what machine could have fashioned a finer afternoon?

HOAR FROST MOON

TO SUGAR BUSH SOLSTICE

A Sure, Quiet Route to Stardom

If it hadn't been for a dog that refused to sleep in the house, I might have never given the stars a second glance. But as a country dog, she'd rather sleep in the barn on a bed of dry straw. To doze in 68-degree comfort on the living room carpet was not for her. Even on a 10-below night, she'd bark, whine, scratch and irritate until I relented. I'd rise with a groan from the comfort of book and chair and we'd make the 50-yard trudge in darkness to her nightly quarters.

What began as a begrudging chore soon grew into an agreeable ritual. I'd empty a cup of dry food into her bowl, and when the barn door thumped shut it marked the proper end of another day. Once outside, I'd pause for the barn prayers: one Pater Noster and five Ave Marias. I'd first done so during a time of sickness and trial and this ritual, too, had stayed with me. I'd face north and Polaris would give its benediction while the dog contentedly crunched her ration.

It was on a cloudless winter night that I first looked in

earnest at the stars. I can't recall why, but for once I saw them for what they really are: deep and remotely silent, the only wilderness left untouched by human hands or desire. Yet the stars also felt close enough to be knowable. Provided that I knew them, which inexcusably, as a self-appointed lay naturalist, I did not. I'd focused on the world underfoot with no thought of the universe overhead. I'd been too absorbed by the ant-farm busyness of my own puny existence to pay the stars any mind.

All I could identify for sure were the Big Dipper and Orion and knowing those two was the intellectual equivalent of playing Chopsticks. As with most modern humans, I suffered from an extreme case of celestial ignorance. Made as we are from stardust, you'd think we'd pay them more heed. But no. Twenty centuries ago, an unlettered, unshod Bedouin shepherd would have known more about stars than almost anyone does today, save astronomers. The blandishments of central heat, electric lights and the lotus-eater seduction of our glowing screens lure us away from the great zodiac wheel of the seasons. We no longer tell myths about the stars or search their depths for signs of ancient prophecies revealed.

So, on that December evening, I resolved to take a giant technological step backwards. I would learn by sight and by name the major constellations in the winter sky.

At first, I tried the obvious 21st century shortcut: a telescope. I'd gotten a discount store model two years earlier and had never seriously used it. Now that I did, it proved a major disappointment. By design, a telescope focuses narrowly on a singular point in space. That's not much help if you want to find an entire constellation, and its position relative to those nearby.

Instead, I used a $10 plastic star chart to unlock the secrets of the visible universe. My wife had given it to me for Christmas and it was perfect. It's made of two movable disks. Turn the top disk to say, 9 p.m., Feb. 2, and the lower disk shows where the constellations stand in the sky.

After supper, I'd swaddle myself in ice-fishing clothes and head to the field behind the barn. We have no yard light, so it's always darkest there. With a tiny red penlight to read the chart, I'd scan the vast canyons of space for patterns in the sky. I was unaccompanied, but never alone. About 9:30 p.m., a band of coyotes would howl and yip from deep in the marsh. A bit later, the tremolo of a screech owl would echo from the little woods across the road. In the way of natural sounds, these added, rather than subtracted, from the winter quietude.

Then after several weeks, I realized something curious that my chart didn't tell me: You can't *hear* the stars, but you must nonetheless listen closely to *see* them.

Such listening isn't done with the ears, but through attenuation of the mind and body. While the time required to reach this state may vary, there does seem to be a common baseline. It takes about 20 minutes for the eyes to adapt to darkness; about 20 minutes for the body's relaxation response to lower breathing rate, stress hormones and blood pressure;

about 20 minutes of brisk walking down a starlit road to reap the calming benefits of exercise.

Not until I stilled myself would the stars — much like black -and-white photos in a dark-room developer's bath — gradually reveal themselves. As my pupils dilated and mental focus sharpened, the naked eye and its wonderful acuity would do the rest. It's almost an autonomous process. The eye wants to find stars because it craves novelty as it does movement; it's forever alert to new patterns and motion, even in the periphery. It's eager to notice not just stars, but bright planets and the pinprick flash of satellites in high orbit.

For me, the best part of stargazing is finding new constellations. When I veer into the complexities of astronomy, I'm soon discouraged by my ineptitude in math and physics. My advice is that each of us make of the stars what we will. They belong to us all; no endowed professorship required. Besides, it's here — humanities majors unite! — that someone who's grounded in myth and literature can understand the stars as legends writ large in the sky.

Now granted, it's scientists who name the constellations these days. That's how we end up with scintillating monikers such as "M-42" in Orion's belt. (Not to be confused with Michigan's M-42 highway or the Army's old M-42 anti-aircraft gun.) Thankfully, the 88 major constellations still recount the epic tales of antiquity. Cassiopeia, for instance, the queen whose raised arms form a wide "W." She was chained to her rocky throne for a vainglorious offense against Poseidon. Or the ubiquitous Big Dipper, which real-life runaway slaves in the 1840s called the Drinking Gourd. They followed it north to freedom on the Underground Railroad. Centuries earlier, the Iroquois and Micmac Indians saw the Big Dipper as the tail of a Great Bear. Look past the image of a dipper and it's easy to see the stars that form the bear's legs and feet. It was the wounded bear's blood, Native Americans said, that made the trees turn scarlet in autumn. If only as a memory aid, I'll take a bloody, spectral bear over an M-40 something star cluster any day.

After you've found one constellation, it usually stairsteps to another. Orion the Hunter, for instance, does more than straddle the southern sky like some celestial version of Notre Dame's Touchdown Jesus. At his feet runs the dog star Sirius and Procyon. Their prey, Lepus the Hare, bounds further to the south. Every child should see Lepus, who wears the only known pair of bunny ears in the galaxy. He definitely deserves his own Pixar movie.

There were other such revelations, small potatoes to anyone but me. I found Auriga, Cepheus, Leo, the Triangulum, the Pleiades, Boötes, Hercules and so on. Within a few weeks, my affinity with these eternally distant blobs of gas felt personal. After the stars were obscured by clouds for a few nights, it felt giddy to see them again. It must've been nights such as these that inspired the booming theophany of Psalm 19: "The heavens declare the glory of God; the skies proclaim the work of his hands ..."

By the time the rains and fog of March came, I could identify 25 constellations. In practical terms, this meant I'd come to know a few dozen of the 2,500 stars visible to an unaided eye. A pittance by astronomer's standards, but not a bad haul for an amateur, I told myself.

However, the last lesson in my stargazer's novitiate was one of the most profound. It's when I learned how much the stars have to teach us about trees and souls.

As was my habit, I studied the roadside trees as I walked. These include the Twin Sisters, two shapely black walnuts, and Old Stubby, a centenarian black oak as shaggy and fierce as a Norse king on his throne. But my favorite was a wizened sycamore that long ago lost its top in some forgotten storm. What remains are two massive, opposite limbs — their brawny arms and knobby elbows fixed upward like those of Moses in the Hebrew battle against the Amalekites. Yet on this night, what caught my eye was how the bright glow of Sirius seemed perched in the sycamore's broken crown. In some inscrutable way, the two appeared connected. It was as if the tree cradled a kindred star — and one 52 trillion miles away, no less — in its woody bosom.

If that sounds like so much misty hokum, then consider this: The tree *was* shaped by a star, as was every tree the world has ever known. Trees are little more than light incarnate. Starlight (sunlight if you prefer) first warms the ground to coax a tree seed from the soil. From there, sunlight shapes the course of its woody ascension upward.

On a winter night, a leafless tree reveals this solar history with special clarity. You might think that the sky overhead would be darker than a tree, but it's not. The trees stand in black silhouette against all else, and with stark purity, leave nothing concealed. The angle and cantilever of every twig, branch and trunk proclaims its fealty to the sun that gave it life. Whichever way it grows, the tree wants nothing more than to follow the light.

It occurred to me that in a spiritual sense, it's much the same with people. We shape our character and destiny by the light and love we turn toward or turn against. Imagine, then, how a soul would look if we saw it profiled like a bare tree against the sky. Would the limbs of pride appear way over-developed, like a bodybuilder who only works his pecs and biceps? Would the branches of generosity look weak and scrawny? I'm afraid that mine would. Yet I also know that as long as we're vertical and taking nourishment, some measure of redirection remains possible. Even an old tree can turn light-ward, once it finds a hopeful new opening in the sky.

Five Ways to Tell if it's Winter in a Michigan Farmhouse

The years have a way of making technology lose its luster and bluster. As do the centuries. When our Michigan farmhouse was built, the latest in online hardware was a Morse Code key. With that, you could've sent a t-mail (telegram) to the White House. It was then occupied by President Abraham Lincoln.

We've lived in our two-story brick home for two decades and have spent more money to renovate it than we did to buy it. Our technology upgrades have been more third-world progressive than first-world impressive. We've added heat registers, electrical outlets, an upstairs toilet, clothes closets and (my favorite) windows that actually open. The old wooden window sashes were painted shut to keep out drafts. This seemed like an idiotic, shortsighted and desperate measure — until I spent my first winter here.

Even now, in some rooms and corners, it still feels like 1864. There's a certain wilderness within that will not be tamed, no matter how we try to refurbish the house into submission. It's a primal force, an indwelling native spirit that refuses to yield. You feel it whenever the hawkish wind keens around the eaves and rattles the 12-pane windows. You see it personified in the tree-trunk floor posts, their bark still on, that stand like petrified sentinels in the cobblestone Michigan basement.

When I was younger, stronger and dumber, I figured to have it all modernized in three, maybe four years tops. Now I know that it's a battle I'll never win — and perhaps am not meant to. As long as I'm here I've decided to leave some regions of the house forever wild. Which is to say cold, dark, dirt-floored, unpainted and congenial to over-wintering rodents. From December to late March, that means the outdoors will often be as close as the next room. Even without a calendar, here's how one knows that winter has arrived:

❋ *You can see your breath in the back living room:*

Officially — ah, the irony — it wasn't called a living room but a summer kitchen. Meals were cooked there during hot weather so that the main kitchen's woodstove wouldn't over-heat the house. Our summer kitchen was built above a dirt-floored crawl space. I went down there once to insulate and got briefly stuck between the hand-hewn timber beams and the bare earth. (It struck me then as the kind of dark, loathsome cavity where a serial killer would hide dismembered body parts.) We've since made it into a comfortable living room and added a cheery, wood-burning fireplace. When it's ablaze, we can raise the temperature to nearly 70. During the week, when there's no fire, temps hover in the upper 20s. The bright side? It's yet to see snow and there's virtually no wind chill.

✻ *Your propane gas bill is higher than the mortgage payment:* Put another way, on a monthly basis the house costs more to heat than to live in. And don't try to sell us on geothermal heat pumps, solar panels, windmills, corn burners, wood pellet burners, methane gas digesters, or outdoor wood-fired boilers like my brother has. For each of these there's tradeoffs (high installation costs) and complicating factors (spend every fall weekend cutting firewood) that make the costs shake out about equally.

The main problem is that you can't insulate a house with solid brick side walls. Our walls are three bricks thick, so once they get cold, they stay cold. Yes, one could affix siding to the outside walls, along with insulation and gypsum board to the interior walls. Except that all these would be harmful to the old brick and aesthetically tacky to boot. Either way, you've got to pay through the nose to keep your feet warm in an old brick house.

51

❈ *The Mouse Drawer has full occupancy:*

To keep all the rodents out of a 19th century farmhouse, you'd need to encase it in blast-proof concrete walls like those around the U.S. Embassy in Baghdad.

Absent that, and because my three indolent cats appear to have struck a non-aggression pact with the Field Mouse Resistance Army, I've become the resident mouser. It's a typical case of asymmetrical warfare. I come equipped with my human hubris and conventional American weaponry — i.e. traps baited with peanut butter (crunchy works better than creamy). The mice, like armed peasants everywhere, know and own the local terrain. I'm just another invading infidel. Meanwhile, their kind has occupied this porous-walled homeland for 160 years.

Once the cold drives the mice indoors, I usually trap six or seven under the kitchen sink. Then after those early defeats, a defiant few retreat to the dreaded Mouse Drawer. It's a narrow rectangle of impregnable high ground just left of the stove, a Khyber Pass where all attempts at homeland defense meet with futility. We do keep some utensils there, but my wife considers them accursed and unclean. Trust me: No measure of disinfection could render them touchable. The icy phrase, "That came from ... the *Mouse Drawer?*" ends all discussion of the topic.

✻ *The storeroom doubles as a refrigerator:*

This one's more a convenience than a detriment. Don't have enough room to cool a six-pack of beer or few liters of pop? Got a big kettle of soup that's still too hot to set in the refrigerator? Or bags of apples, baskets of summer squash, bundles of sweet onions and clumps of dried dill and basil? Then let winter work for you for a change. Transform (probably too lofty a word) your storeroom/mudroom, garage into a walk-in cooler. Yes, you've got to overcome the prudish, bourgeoisie notion that it's unseemly to store edibles next to a volleyball net or rusty toolbox. But is there that much difference between 35 degrees in a refrigerator and 35 degrees in a mudroom? You think the food cares? Besides, we've had no problems out there with mice. They'd rather stay in the main house where it's warm.

✻ *The reign and ruin of the icicle kingdom:*

As earlier mentioned, old houses leak heat the way that scurrilous White House officials leak news tips. And when heat migrates to a cooler surface, it surrenders its latent energy to cause condensation. On a glass of iced tea in June, that process raises those delightful beads of moisture that trickle down to dampen your drink coaster. On a steel roof in January, it melts the snow to form rivulets of distilled water that drip from the eaves and form icicles. Everyone loves the look: elegant cylinders of tapered crystalline that refract the winter sun like fine quartz. Even the melodious drip, drip, drip can be a meditation on a drowsy Sunday afternoon.

Under the right conditions, I've seen icicles that are six feet long and as big around as a girl's waist. That's how big we grow them in the L-shaped crook of our house. And there they hang, stalactites with homicidal intent, perched on the cliffs of catastrophe. Until, at 1 a.m. or so on a foggy March night, they crash and boom to earth like calving icebergs in a Norwegian fjord. Startling in the extreme, but not altogether unwelcome. It's simply the Lord's own water music, come to tell the old house that winter has loosened its icy grip once more.

No Chairlift, No Spandex, No Problem: The Rustic Virtues of X-C Skiing

During the fall color tour, we often drive to a ski resort west of Three Rivers. It's about the only time my family visits the place, which goes by the optimistic name of Swiss Valley (base elevation 975 feet). Its highest ski slope tops out at 1,200 feet, which affords the only 360-degree panorama around. They offer free rides to the top in a four-wheel ATV so leaf peepers can take in the October splendor.

Yet for parents with drill sergeant proclivities, there's another option. They can direct their children to walk up the big hill instead. To do so provides not only a thigh-burning workout, but breathless conversation of a most spirited sort. Here's a snippet of the filial repartee that I've come to expect during the climb.

"This is, by *far*," spat my eldest daughter, a long-legged and extremely fit volleyball player, "the *stupidest* thing you have *ever* made me do."

Maybe it was, but up we went until we bagged the 1,200-footer, smug in the knowledge that our own two legs had propelled us there. With nothing else to prove, we flagged down a four-wheeler and caught a ride to the bottom.

But as we bumped downhill it occurred to me that this approach was all wrong. And not simply because I'd provoked my daughters into a feat of needless exertion — it's my special calling to do that. No, in a larger sense, it was that our cardiovascular defiance had run contrary to the gravitational premise of the place. At a ski resort you're supposed to let machine power take you uphill and then let gravity take you down. And for me, it's precisely this mechanical intrusion that makes downhill skiing such a conflicted enterprise.

While I greatly admire the courage and athleticism of downhill skiers, I can't find much to like about downhill ski resorts. The first turnoff for me is their architecture. They blight the landscape with boxy-bland condos and Monopoly figurine hotels, whose sprawl-friendly design detracts from the heavenly scenery they were built to serve.

Ski resort developers also inflict great trauma on mountains, hills and fragile alpine ecosystems. Acres and acres of native trees and rock forms are bulldozed away in broad, barren swaths to make ski runs. This heavy-handed practice mars the ancient visage of hills and ridgelines. Harsh floodlights, robotic snow machines and looming ranks of steel ski lift towers either complete or desecrate the scene, depending on your point of view. For a sport so rooted in natural elements, ski resorts project an assembly line aesthetic where nature can feel as stage-managed as a miniature golf course.

What's the option for those who'd rather forgo the Orcish overtones of first-world recreational tourism? If you really love downhill skiing, I suppose there isn't one. Nothing can rival its vertical dash, Olympic panache and après ski amenities. To race with abandon through a foot of powder down a 12,000-foot mountainside in Colorado (or even a 1,200-foot hill in southern Michigan) brooks no comparison.

But if you want rigorous exercise, and skiing that's easier on the wallet and the environment, then consider the hyphenated alternative: cross-country skiing.

The main differences between cross-country and downhill skiing involve the equipment and terrain. Cross-country skis are long and narrow. They use boots that connect to the ski at the toes, but leave the heel free to move. This allows the skier to kick-and-glide across level ground or to sidestep up hills and inclines.

On a cross-country ski trail, you meet the landscape on its own terms. It's usually done on a low-impact route through fields and forests that will double as a hiking trail after the snow melts. The sights and sounds of nature are paramount. It's quiet enough to hear the five-note song of a chickadee, or the castanet-rustle of oak leaves in the winter breeze. And wild enough to run over a still-steaming clump of wild turkey poop on the trail.

Our favorite place to ski locally is Love Creek County Park

near Berrien Springs, Michigan. The park is foremost a natural area, with 150 acres of wild habitat and six miles of trails. Love Creek looks and feels like a nature center that happens to rent skis. They issue the equipment ($5 for children, $10 for adults) in a room flanked by tanks of fish, turtles, snakes and salamanders. A wall of floor-length windows faces a beech maple forest. A host of seed and suet feeders are aflutter with evening grosbeaks, blue jays, purple finches, downy woodpeckers and red-headed woodpeckers. It's like a live trailer for the movie that awaits outside.

Of our visits to Love Creek, one outing stands out from the rest. It was the day my wife and I escorted a Christmas break crowd of six cousins, two of whom had no ski experience.

Apart from the rented skis, we had little in the way of outdoorista apparel. Amanda, my niece, sported a second-hand wool overcoat that could've come from the trenches of World War I. Yet her urban Detroit, thrift-store chic fit right in with the fuddy-duddy earnestness that's peculiar to "X-C ski" culture. There were rusticated men with frightening neck beards, for instance, and more than a few women who appeared to have cut their own hair. There were Nordic purists who prefer herringbone knickers and classic wool sweaters (scratchy as medieval hair shirts and reeking of moth balls). There were fashion basket cases, such as myself, who showed up in whatever Dad jeans and faded sweatshirt they pulled on that morning.

Around here at least, the XC ski scene still exudes a certain upright Midwestern propriety. It's the lutefisk and church-potluck ethos that Garrison Keillor once lampooned on public radio. You do see some rainbow sherbet-hued ski wear at places like Love Creek, but nothing like the polyester avalanche at a downhill resort.

With few social distractions, what you mainly do on a cross-country course is ski.

Once outside the nature center, we geared up under a cerulean blue sky dotted with junco-gray clouds. There was no chairlift line (but then there was no chairlift!) and the trail began 20 feet from the building. We set out for the green and yellow "Easy" route, as advised by a park ranger who rightly pegged us for slow movers.

The course lay gentle on the land, little more than a footpath with snow cover. It first dipped down to cross a wooden footbridge over the purling waters of Love Creek. It turned into the woods where it hugged the lip of a heavily timbered ravine. It circled a marsh where a goshawk cruised overhead, eager for some careless vole or rabbit to make a fatal, but providential (for the hawk anyway) mistake.

There was little in the way of heart-throbbing excitement. The modest hills — and you could scarcely call them that — would bestir no downhiller's heart. Nothing much seemed extraordinary, save for the massive and venerable sycamore that we group-hugged for a family photo. We skied some, fell down some, bumped into a few trees and generally ended up tired, but invigorated. We were overheated, but our toes and fingers were numb from the cold. It was, in its own richly subtle way, a peak life experience.

So why did we enjoy it so? What kind of dullard would prefer miles of horizontal sameness to the near-erotic tingle of a downhill run?

The fleeting nature of a holiday gathering had much to do with it. When children are young, family get-togethers are so common that we take them for granted. They sometimes feel compulsory rather than celebratory. Then, before we know it, the entropy of the late teens and 20s pulls our kids away from us. Their orbits become wider, less predictably elliptical. Kuwait. California. Utah. Chicago. For us to meet at the same time and place can become a mathematical impossibility.

The outing at Love Creek surmounted all that. They were home. The park was nearby. It was cheap, it was easy, it was fun. Cross-country skiing, a humble, agreeable sport with a low bar for entry in terms of age, income and ability, had made it so.

There must be others, perhaps ex-downhillers with creaky knees, who would enjoy it just as much. All I can say is give it a chance. Newcomers tend to underestimate the deep, kinetic satisfaction that comes from the kick-pole-glide motion that is the fluid gait of a cross-country skier. It's remarkably intuitive. It's like the sensation that people feel when they paddle a kayak for the first time. And for good reason. A kayak paddle, like a pair of cross-country skis, comes encoded with several millennia of accumulated wisdom and design. It works right, and feels right, because our ancestors perfected the body mechanics eons ago. Their mediums were wood, whale bone and seal skin. Ours are plastics and poly carbons that many of us can't pronounce, much less spell. But the underlying spirit of fluidity and intuitive mobility remains.

When we use skis in a natural setting, we reconnect with their original function: not as a toy for play, but as a means of transport. It's for this reason, 5,000 years ago, that clever Scandinavians invented a tool that leveraged one's arms and legs to glide atop the deep snows of northern Europe. Even today, that's the rationale for cross-country skiing. It's a walk in the winter woods made easier by balance poles, and the long, skinny flat things we strap to our feet.

Finally, there's the lightly trod nature of a cross-country ski trail network itself. It's as ephemeral and seasonal as an Indian hunting camp. Come spring, it will simply vanish with the snow. There'll be few signs at Love Creek (except for some pink trail ribbons) that anyone on skis ever passed this way. In an age when even a well-intended sport like downhill skiing can denude the earth, it's hard to imagine a better way to cross the country than that.

Thea's Feeder: A Feathered Opera in Two Parts

It took the eponymous song of a black-capped chickadee (chick-a-dee-dee-dee, if you must know) to make me go shopping on a Saturday in December. But there he was, in a cold drizzle, hovering around our empty bird feeder. OK, then, compadre. For you I'll break my vow of retail abstinence and stand in line for 15 minutes to buy some bird feed and suet cakes.

Once back home, I sawed off the top of a plastic milk jug to make a poor man's grain scoop. The black oil sunflower seeds sped through it with a satisfying *whish* as I filled our three feeders to the brim. My sentimental favorite is the one that a friend and fellow writer, Thea Lapham, bought us as a wedding gift. It's nothing fancy. Just a clear acrylic tower with a pitched roof and landing board made of Michigan cedar. Yet in a season when we often buy pointless gifts for people who don't need them, a bird feeder stands out as a worthy exception.

We put out feeders from early December to late March and probably run 150 pounds of seed through them. You can't help but feel good about yourself after you've filled one. It's what biologists call a symbiotic relationship. The birds get some extra protein to endure the cold, and we get a little feathered opera outside our windows.

In the evening, sometimes I'll think about the birds as I doze in my reading chair next to the fireplace. It's a comfort to imagine them asleep under a snowy spruce bough, the furnace of their tiny hearts fueled by the good seed that will keep them warm and alive till morning. Such is the altruistic nature of a birdfeeder. You can buy one for yourself, or for a friend, but the feeder can only be used in service of another creature. Selfishness doesn't become it.

For the first nine years that we fed birds, I didn't think much about why. They looked pretty and had a voracious appetite, which seemed reason and reward enough. It gave me a proprietary pleasure to care for them. It must've been how my mother felt when she watched her six-foot sons wolf down mountains of mashed potatoes and meat loaf. But we had nothing on the average songbird. Researchers at Cornell say that a 150-pound human would need to eat 61,853 calories per day to match the 10-calorie intake of a half-ounce chickadee.

Then came the year when the birds decided to take care of me for a while. It was February, ruthlessly cold. For reasons that in hindsight seem blatantly obvious, I'd worked myself into a state of exhaustion — mental, physical, spiritual, you name it. Work had become a fixation that left me too tired to rest or recuperate. Both my body and my doctor demanded that I take two months of sick leave.

Part of my recovery required that I practice something called the Relaxation Response. Essentially, you're supposed to sit in a quiet room with your eyes closed and think peaceful thoughts. That's fine, provided you have thoughts you'd like to think about. I did not, so I'd open my eyes and focus on something less disturbing ... like the bird feeder.

Sometimes, after I zoned out for a half-hour or so, I'd glimpse an alternate reality. I began to see the feeder as more than a humble small grain dispenser. It was instead a nexus of fluid energy and calculated motion. The birds would ascend and descend, angelic in form and manner, like earthly seraphs around a lesser throne. They'd come and go with a pattern you could almost discern.

One afternoon, as I watched in a pharmaceutical haze, I recalled the story of "Papillon," a popular book and movie from my youth. "Papillon" was a memoir (some say fiction) that was based on the life of Henri Charrière. After Charrière was wrongly accused of murder in his native France, he was sent to an "inescapable" prison on Devil's Island, off the coast of French Guiana in South America.

Papillon, who was so named for the butterfly tattoo on his chest, spent 19 months in solitary confinement on Devil's Island. He was no scientist, yet he studied nature closely enough to make a most useful discovery. Namely, that every seventh wave was large enough to sweep a person out to sea. Using a sack of coconut husks for a raft, he and another prisoner dove from a high cliff into the foamy maelstrom of waves below. After several harrowing days at sea beneath a blowtorch tropical sun with nothing but coconut husks to eat, they made landfall on a beach in French Guiana. More adventures ensued — the other escapee fell into quicksand and died — but Papillon would find freedom, fortune and eventual celebrity in Venezuela.

As for me, I was under self-imposed house arrest, with no coconut raft in sight.

Yet while birds don't offer much in the way of career guidance, stare long enough and their tranquility does creep up on you. It's a bit like stargazing without a telescope. With the naked eye, stars are most visible when viewed with peripheral, instead of straight-on vision. That's because the eye's periphery has an abundance of rod cells, which are well suited for light detection. The eye's center, which has more cone cells, is better suited for color detection. The action around my feeder was similar to that. I needed to sneak up on the birds sideways before they'd reveal their secrets. Too bad my family medical leave expired before I figured it all out.

These were the kind of half-baked theories that Thea and I (she'd given us the bird feeder) loved to discuss over lunch. And Lord, how she loved to talk. She had a blue jay way of cocking her head as she spoke, nodding for dramatic effect as if to crack a stubborn nut. This mannerism, it must be said, was the only thing bird-like about her. Thea had a big heart, big voice, big body; she was a tireless newspaper reporter and overall nonstop force of nature. Unstoppable, at least, until the end. She was taken by uterine cancer at age 53.

The last time I saw Thea, she went on and on about her plans to write a book titled "I Don't Have Time for This." Those were the first words out of her mouth when she learned of her terminal diagnosis. She lived them to the end, and as befits a good journalist, never had to ask for a retraction.

Last season, for the first time in 16 years, I gave the cedar trim on Thea's feeder a coat of tung oil to prolong its life. It's a hopeful gesture, and "Hope," wrote Emily Dickinson, "is the thing with feathers that perches in the soul."

Neither Thea nor I, ink-stained wretches that we are, would ever dare write something that poetic. But I can understand why a fellow shut-in like Dickinson would want to. May wild birds give flight to all that Thea would have me say.

The Sweet, Slippery Path
to Success

If trees can ponder such matters, then the sugar maples of Russ Forest must have felt unloved and forgotten. For 55 years, they'd waited faithfully, demure in their cloaks of silvery gray, like shy country girls who never get asked to the prom.

Their native sweetness might still be unrequited if weren't for Sandy Wiseman. It wasn't until 2000 that Wiseman, a teacher and counselor, finally looked out with new eyes from the little school next door.

Wiseman wanted to develop a hands-on project for her economics class at Volinia Outcomes School. Yet when she consulted with the experts in Lansing, they suggested she open a stationery store. This, in Volinia, Michigan, a crossroads of maybe 100 people that's nine miles from Marcellus (pop. 1,191). This, in a region dotted with hog farms — enterprises

with a decidedly low demand for deckled envelopes and calligraphy pens.

"Stationery? Well, that's boring," Wiseman said. "There's
must be *something* these kids can do here."

That something was the rank upon rank of long-neglected
maples. As a U.P. native, Wiseman knew what a sugar bush
looked like. And behold: There was a fine one staring back at
her through the classroom windows.

"I called Michigan State University (which owns Russ
Forest) and they said they'd planted 700 maple trees in 1946
for a sugaring operation," Wiseman recalled. "But no one had
ever used the trees for that. So, they agreed to lease it to us
for a $1 per year."

And so began the unlikely saga of Volinia Maple. To the
school's knowledge, it's the only student-run maple sugaring
operation in Michigan and maybe anywhere. Students tap the
trees, haul the sap, boil it into syrup and each year sell all they
produce. On the last Saturday in March, they hold a pancake
breakfast with guided tours and horse-drawn wagon rides
through the sugar bush. Some years they attract 1,000 visitors. All this in a school that's small even by rural standards:
about 100 students in grades 7-12.

From the start, the school board said Volinia Maple would
have to pay its own way. That didn't faze Wiseman, an entrepre-
neur who had started and ran several businesses. She applied
for and received a $17,000 grant from the Edward Lowe Foun-
dation in nearby Cassopolis, a philanthropy started by the
man who invented kitty litter. The money paid for the sugar-

ing equipment, while Northrop Logging in Marcellus donated lumber for the sugarhouse (where syrup is made) and two local carpenters volunteered to build it. By winter 2001, the inaugural sugaring season was underway.

Volinia Maple has since established itself as a program that not only pays for itself but earns enough profit to pay for student field trips. (Do high school football teams ever end up in the black?) All this at an alternative school, which some consider the last stop for kids who are hell-bent for juvenile detention or jail unless they turn over a new leaf. Or sap bucket.

"We get kids who are headed down the wrong path and this can totally turn them around," said Volinia principal Don Price, who took over the maple project when Wiseman retired in 2009. "It actually makes them better students. They know they've got to keep their grades up if they want to work in the woods."

From the outset, Volinia Maple's real genius was how it tied into the school's curriculum. It was all of one piece: language arts, math and science. Students could write English papers about maple syrup, whose history traces to the local Potawatomi. They could build a website and create marketing materials to sell their products. They could study the science of syrup — its botany and chemistry — and the weather conditions that predict peak sap flow. To hone public speaking skills, they'd give presentations to service and business clubs like the Rotary. As a real-life application of business math, they designed a bookkeeping system.

This is a story, for almost anyone who hears it, that's beyond good news.

Doesn't Volinia Maple, with its common-sense blend of work experience and relevant instruction, make you want to shout *Hallelujah!* to the rooftops? It makes you wonder why no one thought of this before. It makes you wish for Volinias that baked bread, raised catfish, made pottery or built sturdy, low-cost furniture. It makes you hope that such a novel program could continue without meddling from the state's educational hegemony.

If only that were the case.

After a two-year absence, my family and I made the rolling, 25-minute drive to Volinia Maple Fest at Russ Forest. The reasons were twofold. My girls were hungry for real maple syrup (they'd outgrown the plasticized unreality known as Mrs. Butterworth's) and I needed an easy, feel-good topic to write about for my newspaper column.

The breakfast ran from 7 a.m. to 12:30 p.m., but when we arrived at 10:45 a.m. the crowd had thinned. Still, the Volinia Maple Fest flyers were cheery as ever, heavy on the adjectival exhortation that you'd expect from high school marketers. They promised "*Juicy* Sausage! *Fluffy* Pancakes! *Tasty* Orange Juice!"

We sat down in the gym to enjoy the feast's namesake condiment on our pancakes and scrambled eggs (maple syrup: the thinking man's ketchup). I've been to other maple syrup festivals where they're stingy on samples. You get a few meager drops dabbed on a Popsicle stick. At Volinia, you help yourself to bottles of their syrup that sit generously on every table.

This year, though, the bottled syrup was on sale in the gym where breakfast was served. It was the first sign that something was amiss.

"How come you're selling it here instead of at the store?" I asked a teacher who managed the cash box.

"The store?" she said. "Well, we only use that to stage our equipment now."

Not good, if only for stylistic reasons. The cozy old store had beadboard wainscoting, maple-leaf wallpaper and a bank of bright windows that overlooked Gards Prairie Road. A description thereof was supposed to account for 150 words of my 750-word column. A few comments from an eager student who led sugar bush tours would use up another 150. A quote from a teacher, a little Volinia Maple history, and some adjectival exhortation of my own about demure, silvery gray maples would fill the rest.

We went outside to the sugar shack, but there was no one there. The evaporator was drained and idle. Full sap buckets hung from the trees, frozen solid into milky white cylinders. The student-led tours were done for the day. Were we late or had the Maple Fest, quite literally, run out of steam?

The root cause, I feared, was more than a March cold snap. I suspected a phenomenon that often afflicts promising start-up nonprofits such as Volinia Maple. It's called *founder's syndrome*. It sets in when (a.) the first blush of novelty subsides (b.) the popular leader who started the organization departs; and (c.) a new leader arrives without the means or interest to keep things going. The fact that Michigan had changed its state curriculum hadn't helped any.

The next day, a phone call to Don Price confirmed some of the above.

"Yeah, we had to drop the economics class when the teaching position was eliminated," Price explained. "That's why we no longer call it a student-run business. It's become a school project instead."

Gone, too, he said, was the brilliantly integrated curriculum. In its place was Michigan's new standardized curriculum. Suffice to say it had no maple trees in it. None of which boded well for the puff piece I wanted to write. With a column deadline looming, I scheduled one more visit to at least get some student color into the story.

"Hey, we're making syrup today," hailed Price, as I walked up to the sugarhouse. Here it was, Good Friday morning, and the temperature probably wouldn't clear freezing.

Price, who looked to be in his early 40s, wore faded jeans with a brown sweater. He was tall and soft-spoken, with a bald pate and the slight stoop of an athlete just past his prime. Behind him stood what he called the heart of his operation. And it wasn't Volinia's high-end evaporator, the fuel oil-fired dynamo that made corkscrews of sweet steam twirl up through the clerestory peak. No, the two big cogs were 17-year-old juniors Tim Wegner and Austin Owens.

Instead of the old economics class, which had up to 15 students, these guys were it. From tap to table, they would ensure the syrup's overall safety, quality and consistency. On their shoulders rested the present and near future of Volinia Maple.

"I didn't know anything about maple syrup when I started last year, except that it tasted good," said Wegner, above the evaporator's frothy roar.

"Now, in one day we cook down about 300 gallons of sap. There, it just hit 217 degrees," he said, pointing to a red LED sensor. "It's pretty much automated, but you'll burn a batch of syrup if you don't watch it."

The sugar shacks of old offered moderate comfort from open wood fires that heated the evaporators. Syrup tenders would sleep on cots to keep the fires going overnight. The modern version is ice-cave cold, with a bare concrete floor that would make a penguin's feet go numb. I can't imagine how frigid it must be in the pre-dawn darkness. But the crew's other half can.

"I get up at 4 a.m. so I can be here by 5," says Owens, a lanky redhead who lives with his grandfather. "But we're lucky. Who else gets to make syrup every day?"

Minutes later, like quail flushed from a fencerow, a covey of seven or eight students rushed from the school to the sugar shack. They bounced up with the loose-jointed energy you'd expect from teenagers on the lam from schoolwork. A few started to horse around by the equipment, but sugar boss Wegner would have none of it.

"You guys need to get out there and empty sap buckets," he said firmly.

It was sunny, in the mid-20s, but the sap pails were clogged with discs of ice an inch thick. How to get it off? With your bare hands. While immersed in a sub-freezing ice bath. But no rubber gloves for Volinia kids; they say it slows them down. And no complaining, either, as they trudged with their loads to the sugar house.

From February on, they'll make thousands of such trips to the 700 trees. They dump the pails into 50-gallon plastic barrels that are then pulled — they weigh 200-300 pounds apiece — by a two-wheeled handcart to the sugar house. It's manual labor of a sort most American teens haven't done for generations. If it weren't for their saggy jeans and ear studs, you'd swear the Volinia kids were Amish.

Then, as quickly as they appeared, the students fled back inside.

My own fingers were too cold at this point to take notes, so I also went inside the school for a last chat with Price. Here, away from youthful ears, Price shed new light on how this remarkable, premier program was forced to adapt or die.

"Yeah, I'd like to re-start the business class some day and involve more students with everything," Price said. But he also saw one drawback to the old arrangement. Should it again become a formal class, participation would be *mandatory* (a word that sounds as grim when it prefixes maple sugaring as it does colonoscopy).

"When you force kids to work," he said, with masterful

understatement, "I've found that it doesn't always work as well."

Instead, Price had reshaped the program around what could be called the Tom Sawyer School of Motivational Psychology. In "The Adventures of Tom Sawyer," young Tom famously outsources the painting of his Aunt Polly's picket fence. He was able to make the chore seem so appealing that his friends paid him ("... six fire-crackers, a kitten with only one eye, a dead rat...") for the right to do the work. It was all in how he teed it up:

> *"Like it?" said Tom, when asked about fence paint-ing by his pal Ben Rogers. "Well, I don't see why I oughtn't to like it. Does a boy get a chance to white-wash a fence every day?"*

Volinia students must likewise earn the right to tote heavy sap buckets in the 15-degree gloom of a February morning. They must prove themselves worthy to drag the 200-lb. hand-carts over bumpy trails rutted with ice, mud and snow. Only those who behave in class and keep their grades up can par-take of this special privilege.

How does Price pull it off? Not the way many teachers and coaches would do it, with whistles, clipboards, bellowed threats and rule-bound scrutiny. Price (he's got a second job as athletic director for Marcellus schools!) manages with an easy touch. Then, much like trees in a well-thinned forest, his kids grow straight and true when given ample space and light to do so.

Take Austin Owens. It was his idea to arise at 4 a.m. and learn the craft of sugaring. He'd set his mind to it, and perhaps for the first time in a life not marked by school success, had succeeded at something valuable. Every amber ounce of the season's harvest had passed through his hands. Owens had not only proved himself, but had possibly saved himself. And this was adult work, it must be said, not a boy's game played indoors in gaudy polyester shorts.

No less intriguing is Volinia Maple's self-styled succession plan. It's built on the radical notion that teenagers will show up and work hard for free. Each year, Price handpicks the next year's trainees. They must apprentice themselves to mentors such as Wegner and Owens. They will learn syrup-making through toil, taste, touch and smell. How it drips from steel spiles into the bucket, splashes with a viscous glug into the outdoor holding tanks and throttles like an amber river through the evaporator. They will spend winter days infused by coronas of sweet steam and, should they live to be 100, they will never, ever tire of its fragrance and smoky-sweet flavor.

"This," said Wegner, with probity rare for any 17-year-old, "is like a family heirloom. We'll make sure that we leave it in good hands."

Volinia Maple now complements the school's academic studies. It still teaches work ethics, science, marketing and public speaking, but there are no grades involved. The sugarhouse was empty on Maple Fest Saturday because the boys had already worked 20 hours that week.

For all that, there's one other crucial element that's an ongoing partner in this operation: Russ Forest itself. It's a silent partner, especially the 120-acre grove of virgin hardwoods that lies due west of the school and sugar bush. The stand is renowned for its massive tulip poplars, some with trunks as wide across as a pitcher's mound. It was preserved in the mid-19th century by pioneer George Newton, who had the foresight to protect primeval forest at a time when other white settlers were hell-bent on its destruction. Newton, who served in the Michigan House of Representatives, also had the good taste to build an Italianate-style country villa, now restored as a public museum.

The grove's mossy beneficence and monastic quiet holds the little cloister of the school and sugarhouse in its lee. The old trees, I believe, impart a measure of unspoken peace on children who come here from lives of un-peacefulness. It's a pervading and palpable force, even if you never venture into the Big Woods. In its shadow, kids can thrive who should not by tending to trees as others would not. These two negatives create a positive; a reality not lost on those who see in Volinia a model for other schools to follow.

As we were about to leave Maple Fest that Saturday, a team of draft horses clopped in from the last wagon tour. The 10-minute circuit had taken them through the sugar bush.

It was a smooth then bumpy ride that gyrated, like the bipolar spirit of March itself, between blustery snow flurries and lemony shafts of joyful sun. In the way of well-trained horses, the team knew their workday at Volinia was done. They snorted and shuffled their pie plate-sized feet, their leather harnesses damp with salty lather and rich with the earthy scent of horse.

"I just *love* that smell," said a woman, as she reached up to stroke a broad equine forehead. As well she should. On that morning, to profess one's love for the aroma of sweat-soaked horse — no less than Fluffy Pancakes and Fresh Maple Syrup from the trees next door — was a perfect compliment to complement the day.

Hail Sycamore:
Witness of Winter's Light

In the virgin forests of the Midwest, there once grew hardwoods of such enormity that the words "big tree" can scarcely describe them.

Of these, none rivaled the sycamore. The most gigantic stood in the black-muck bottoms of storied rivers such as the Ohio, Mississippi, Wabash, Maumee, Kankakee and St. Joseph. One famous specimen on the Ohio, measured by George Washington, was 13 feet in diameter and 44 feet in circumference.

Such trees were the size of a modest living room. Since big sycamores are often hollow in the middle, settlers would live inside them until a log cabin could be built. Then they'd convert the still-living sycamore into a leafy stable to house pigs, chickens, cows or horses.

This was an age when land was cheap and virgin forest viewed as an unholy obstacle to progress. As settlers drained swamps to make farmland, low-value trees like sycamores became high-profile targets. To dispatch them, pioneers used a technique known as windrowing. It was every bit as rapacious as the slash-and-burn techniques used by avaricious loggers in the Amazon rain forests of today. L.D. Watkins described the carnage in his circa 1900 book "Destruction of the Forests of Southern Michigan."

> *"The huge forest trees were chopped off partly in such a manner that they would fall obliquely towards the center. Then at the end of the line, a huge tree was felled. As it came thundering down on the row of partly fallen trees, they would go down one after another. It was like a battle of giants, a sight of grandeur with a paralyzing roar of sound.*

> *"The trees were left as they had fallen until they were very dry, and when the wind was just right, they were set on fire. The beautiful old forest trees became nothing but huge blackened logs with burial mounds of upturned roots."*

The largest of these trees could've been 500-800 years in the making.

I'm not sorry that I missed the pioneer scourge of malaria or the bed bug-infested cabins. Or, the grisly specter of a 19th century backwoods doctor as he yanked an abscessed tooth from some poor settler's mouth with a pair of rusty pliers.

But it's a pity we'll never get to see those magnificent, unde-filed stands of hardwood timber.

It also raises some questions that I've long puzzled over. Why did these men and women so completely and ruthlessly clear-cut every single old-growth stand in St. Joseph County, Michigan? Within its 333,000-acre borders, couldn't they have saved even one acre of virgin forest? Their annihilation shows an animus for wilderness — which many settlers professed to love — that's coldly unyielding in its brutality.

But what's done is done. Until our protected forests can pile on a few centuries of growth, a big tree aficionado needs to enjoy what's at hand. For that, we're fortunate to have the Big Tree Registry, which lists the size and location of more than 100 state-record species. I, for one, love it. It's something only a rabble of volunteers, afflicted with an arcane passion that would bore the bejeezus out of anyone else, could create. Through the Registry, I learned that Michigan's champion sycamore stands five miles south of Berrien Springs. There was no question but that I had to visit it.

On a Saturday morning in February, we lit out west from Three Rivers on M-60 after my daughter's basketball game. By the time we'd reached Cassopolis, Nancy was drowsy, so I turned off the radio and let her rest. (The thrill of an hour's drive with a middle-aged man to visit an old tree in 10-degree weather had taxed her considerably.) The drive became a sol-itary meditation through a landscape buried deep in pillowed drifts, piled high from one of the snowiest winters on record.

Once we hit the Berrien County back roads, you could tell this was big sycamore country. Past rolling vineyards and orchards, wherever a creek or marsh enfolded a little copse of woods, there you'd see a hulking sycamore.

Their squat lower trunks were barked in flaky, chocolate brown. At chest height, they forked into multiple trunks of elephant-leg proportions. From there on up, their bark faded from mottled, creamy green to ivory or purest white. Piebald, you'd call it, if the same look appeared on a horse.

We found the record tree on a wedge of state land bordered by U.S. 31, a highway overpass and a cul de sac. It was huge, stout and wide-across-the-beam in a grandmotherly kind of way. (With apologies to my stout and departed grandmother). It stood 120 feet tall and measured seven feet in diameter, with a circumference of 21.5 feet. That's only half the size of the behemoth that caught George Washington's eye along the Ohio. But as Michigan's reigning champion it still merits a pilgrimage. Maybe a picnic on the first warm Sunday in May, when Easter egg-yellow dandelions brighten the spring-green grass. Everyone could pose for a Christmas card-worthy photo, their arms and legs akimbo around Grandma Sycamore's ample waist. Trees wait years for that kind of affirmation.

Yet let me also say this: Something about the old tree felt lonely. With its brethren gone, the sycamore had only a self-absorbed subdivision and disinterested freeway for company. This, for a gregarious species that prefers to grow in stately groves along languid rivers.

The finest stand of sycamores I've ever seen grows along Sugar Creek in Turkey Run State Park, Indiana. They dominate the prime waterfront real estate. In their bulky eminence they seem to say, "Yes, we are the sycamore monarchy. As for you, silver maple and basswood, there's room for your common kind inland. Now, you plebeians, be off with you..."

Still, as a landmark tree, a lone sycamore can offer much in the way of spiritual comfort and ecological instruction. Their oddly peeling bark and piebald visage makes them a curiosity, even for those who don't give trees much thought. Their fallen leaves, although a plain and dusty brown, can be as big as a dinner plate. Much like the tree itself, they'll dwarf all others in a fall leaf collection.

After their leaves have fallen, all trees display the naked scaffold of their trunk and branches. Yet while barren oaks and maples do have a muted elegance, few would regard winter as their finest hour. Not so the sycamore. Only in winter can the full beauty of its trunk and crown stand revealed. More so than any other tree, the sycamore exults in winter's light — and thereby stands as a cheerful witness during the coldest, shortest days of the year.

In chameleon fashion, the sycamore's high branches reflect and glorify whatever rays the winter sun provides. At sunrise, they may glow a faint orange. On an overcast day, their white appears as dove gray. As daylight wanes, they take on the violet hue of late afternoon snow. Then, on those rare, lapis lazuli blue-sky days of winter, the sycamore transforms into a being that seems more worthy of heaven than of earth.

Its sun-washed crown glows a dazzling, rapturous white. No seaside beacon on a rocky promontory ever shone with more clarity.

A sycamore of such lineage greeted me each morning along the Kalamazoo River south of Battle Creek. I could see it from nearly a mile off. It was the favorite landmark of my 45-minute commute. It's not especially big — two feet in diameter at most. It's where it stands and what it stands for that makes it exemplary. For this sycamore has borne witness to an environmental holocaust. The tree rises above waters that, in July 2010, suffered the largest inland oil spill in U.S. history. Some 900,000 gallons of Athabasca tar sands crude flooded into the river after an Enbridge pipeline burst upstream near Marshall.

I well recall the sulfurous, Gehenna stench of that day. The oil fumes seeped through my closed car windows, even at a distance of two miles from the river. Next came the turgid, slimy current. Then the bloated fish, blackened turtles, ducks, birds, herons, mink and muskrat. All befouled by human hubris, and the broken promises that attend our reliance — *my* reliance — on this bedeviled fossil fuel.

At the sycamore's base, a gravel parking lot and boat landing served for two years as a marshalling point for the cleanup. It's no place for a beautiful tree … but then an innocent Michigan river is no place for an oil spill.

The Enbridge trucks and airboats are long gone. The $1-billion cleanup, as legally mandated, was completed. I'm not sure if they took pains to protect the sycamore, but at least they did it no apparent harm. It appears unsullied and, as befits royalty, has held itself aloof from the whole tawdry debacle. It lives on to do what its kind has always done: provide shelter for any human or beast who will gently partake of its sprawling hospitality.

PRAIRIE SMOKE

TO LILAC BLOOM

39 Bottles of Wine by the Road, 39 Bottles of Wine ...

There's an otherwise scenic country road near our home that holds great appeal for connoisseurs of cheap wine. And not just any wine, but Arbor Mist. While I've never drank any, I do know this much. It costs around $4 a bottle, rarely shatters on impact and comes in 12 tooty fruity flavors that eventually all smell like putrid Kool Aid.

Now there's no reason to feel morally superior because your tastes run toward $20 bottles of merlot with a real cork instead of a screw cap. What's more, when times are hard, there's a legitimate need for some cheap happy. Mix in a little slow dance and Michigan might even achieve positive population growth.

No, my grievance concerns the containers that all this cheap happy comes in. If this year is like the last, we can expect a shiny harvest once the March rains melt the roadside snow. On a family walk last spring, we picked up 39 empty Arbor

Mist bottles — 39! — that lay scattered along a two-mile stretch. We'd brought along two empty trash bags, but they got so heavy and foul-smelling that we had to get the car to lug them home.

After some initial grousing, the kids made a game of it. They'd chant "Ar-bor *Mist*, Ar-bor *Mist*, Ar-bor *Mist!*" until they found another dead soldier. They also kept track of the most popular varieties. Like a truck stop sommelier, my youngest daughter's vocabulary now includes the terms Exotic Fruit and Sangria Zinfandel (which won hands-down). However, the moldy dregs she found inside the bottles may make her swear off adult beverages forever.

There was also ample time during the cleanup to discuss the sad truth behind this litter. These were not all picnic castoffs from a summer of country love. Not with 39 of them.

No, this was more likely the regular route of a solitary drunk; his via dolorosa, or highway to hell if you prefer the vernacular. It's a grim business, and once you're lured this far down the road, there's no pleasure in it. The party's long been over. It's just drink, drive, toss out the window and repeat as necessary.

Along with the wine empties, we found some harder stuff. There were half-pint plastic bottles of cheap schnapps and tequila, along with quarts of malt liquor, still wrapped in their fugitive brown paper sacks.

The corporations that make this stuff are evilly adept at exploiting the demographics of working-class despair. Feeling socially downtrodden? They'll sell you a product buoyed by advertising that's bold, powerful and virile. It's rife with images of raging bulls, phallic locomotives and melon-chested women airbrushed to soft-porn perfection. Perversely enough, anyone who regularly glugs a bottle of schnapps will render themselves ever less bold, powerful and virile. (I once saw a friend thus destroyed.) The numbers of silent, suffering servants must be legion. My local convenience store devotes more shelf space to cheap booze than to any other item. No fresh lettuce or bananas, but they do have six flavors of addict-friendly vodka.

Still, the roadside cleanup made for good physical and civic exercise. Apart from picking up their rooms — festooned with gym clothes whose bacterial count may rival a fetid Arbor Mist bottle — I don't think we'd ever asked our kids to clean up someone else's mess.

It was, as they pointed out, exceedingly *unfair*. And that's exactly why it made such good practice for adulthood. Soon enough, they'll be asked to clean up many larger messes that were not of their own making. An insolvent Social Security system (Oops, sorry kids!); several intractable Mideast wars; and, closer to home, billions of plastic shopping bags that flutter in the trees near Walmart like so many polyethylene seagulls. Should they choose the vocation of parenthood, there will be the dank surprises that lurk inside several years' worth of loaded diapers. Someday, they may even have to care for an incontinent father who is similarly attired.

But I've noticed that the louder kids complain about an arduous hike or household chore, the more they relish the memory afterward. That certainly proved true here. After their parent-mandated community service, the girls sounded a bit boastful about what we'd accomplished. A little of that's fine by me, though. If someone trashes your home ground, they can't tell you to put a cork in it.

A New Life for an Old Pit

A gravel pit doesn't usually get a second chance at life, financially or socially. Because after you've dug and trucked away all the sand, stone and clay what's left? Mainly a big gash in the earth. The kind that will forever attract heaps of used tires and wrecked cars, much in the way that castoff French fries attract seagulls in a McDonald's parking lot.

Not so, however, the old gravel pit on Hoffman Road in Three Rivers. For it has been reborn in a way that I once thought impossible. It has turned its greatest liability — a post-industrial, bomb-crater landscape — into its greatest asset. What was once a hardscrabble place where blue-collar types went to work, has become a playground where fitness adventurers come to work out. That said, what hasn't changed is my unresolved family conflict with the place, which has been 110 years and 5,000 miles in the making. Which we will unpack shortly.

I first saw the re-imagined pit on a Saturday morning in mid-

March, when I came to cover its grand opening for the local newspaper. The Pit Fitness Ranch — now its official name — was hosting the Frozen Fat Tire Fat Bike Relays, which drew entrants from Michigan, Indiana and Ohio. They competed in a series of 10- to 50-mile relays on a ½-mile dirt track that wound across 50 bumpy acres. Although with temperatures in the low 40s, there was nothing frozen about it. The whole place was soon a slushy mess, which made the bikers love it all the more.

"This is the first race of its kind in the Midwest," said Jamie Stafne, from Heart Smart Events in Marcellus, Michigan, who organized the program with business partner Mark Wright from Three Rivers. "We let the bikers get close to nature and take it as it comes. That's what Heart Smart Events are all about."

It looked like an adult recess, with grownups sprung from garages where they'd tinkered all winter on their carbon fiber derailleurs and titanium bike frames. Bright banners flapped in the wind from sponsors that sold beer coolers and lawn equipment. There was cold beer, hot corn dogs and a warming tent that no one needed because the riders were already ruddy-faced with cheer. Quite hilariously, their backsides were skunk-striped with brown mud, as if they'd been stricken with dysentery on the Oregon trail.

As much as the race, it was the rebirth of the gritty maintenance garage that I found most remarkable. As a teenager, I'd swept its concrete floor with oil-dry to soak up spills from trucks and tractors. Now, the big trucks were long gone —

along with the time clock, girlie calendars, racks of dusty parts and hidden fifth of Canadian Club. There was, instead, a yoga studio (!) with a high-gloss epoxy floor. The room smelled of varnished wood and lemongrass soap. The once-dark garage was bright with natural light, thanks to new windows that overlooked the spring-fed pond. And the studio was staffed *by women*, whose presence was rare, if not implicitly banned, at the old pit.

As for the Fat Tire Bike Race, it's only the beginning. Next will come an 8,000-foot structure to serve devotees of a slightly mad training regimen known as CrossFit. "We've got nearly 400 acres when you count the former Kerr Trust property to the east," said Brock Yost from Three Rivers, who manages the enterprise. "It has woods, ponds and trees, and we'll use it for all kinds of non-motorized activities like foot races and bike races."

And that's the big takeaway: an abandoned gravel pit, a derelict hulk of extractivist 1950s infrastructure, now recycled for sustainable ends. With the heavy equipment gone, the trampled soil will gradually rebound over time. Under the circumstances, a rural community like Three Rivers couldn't ask for more.

That said, there's one thing that time can't heal, absent another Ice Age. Never again will we see "the knobs" in their pre-gravel pit glory.

I first read about the knobs in a collection of columns written by Chet Shafer, a local newsman with a national following. Shafer had a droll, Will Rogers-like style, and wrote for

The Detroit News and The Saturday Evening Post during the 1930s and '40s.

In one of his few poignant essays, Shafer wrote of two widowers on Thanksgiving morning. Shafer saw them at the corner café where he went to drink coffee and drum up story ideas. This time, the usually wisecracking Shafer captured the pathos of the situation. While Shafer was biding time until an afternoon dinner with family, the widowers had nowhere else to go. So, on a day that rang festive for everyone else, they were bound for the knobs to cut firewood in the frosty quiet of the woods. To hear a crosscut saw sing through the trunk of a felled black oak would have to bring comfort enough.

Geologically, the knobs are morainal hills made from the sandy, stony remnants of glaciers. They extend about 10 miles in a broken line from Newberg Township in the south to Flowerfield Township in the north. But it's in the knobs west of Three Rivers where my history intersects with the legacy of my great-grandparents. While both of us sought to earn a decent living there, our impact couldn't have been more different. Where my ancestors had planted and nurtured, I would dig and despoil the very terrain they held dear.

When I came to the pit in 1977, my teenage wants were simple enough. I just needed a job to earn money for beer and gasoline. I lived at home then, as befit a C- student with zero prospects for college or career on the horizon. At age 17, two days after high school graduation, I hired on as a laborer at the pit. The business was then called DeBoer Materials. They mined gravel and stone and produced their own bargain-grade variety of asphalt. (Trade secret revealed: Gravel pit sand is a much cheaper ingredient for asphalt than tar).

My job there was the chain gang version of an eight-hour CrossFit workout. It was grimy and exhausting, a mini-mum-wage crucible to be endured with pick and shovel in the bitumen-steam swirl of 300-degree asphalt. It didn't help that I wore tight Levi's bellbottoms, and cheap vinyl work boots whose crepe soles turned mozzarella gummy in the tarry heat. And the work was even harder on the landscape. On rare days when I got to drive a truck, I'd load up with five yards of material ... and that much more of the knobs would roll down the road forever.

As for my great-grandparents, their arrival was far more cin-ematic. They were swept here on the immigrant tidal wave of the early 20th century. For them, the humble knobs may well have been the God-lit summits of Canaan. That's a little overblown, but not much. They were ethnic Germans who had traveled 5,000 miles from Cseb, Hungary (now Čelarevo, Serbia). The clan patriarch John Mayer arrived first, followed 18 months later by his wife Marianna and their two children. For seven years they bounced between jobs and houses in central Michigan. When John heard of an opening for a "bright young shoemaker" in Three Rivers, the die was cast. In 1910, they bought a cramped, rundown house on 40 acres that backed up to the knobs on Coon Hollow Road. Through endless remodeling and expansion, their home would yield an increase in love, family, faith and homegrown apples for 37 years running.

Growing up, I must've known more about my great-grandparents than most kids did. In the 1960s, my mother had pecked out a lively account of their family history on a manual Smith Corona typewriter. But it wasn't until I visited the pit two years ago — before it became The Pit — that I realized the cruel irony of my role there.

It was a For Sale sign that piqued my interest. I assumed that another aggregate company would soon move in and start mining again. Before the gravel wars began anew, I wanted to see what 10 years of inactivity had brought. What I found heartened me. I fished in the pond and caught and released a half-dozen bluegills that clearly hadn't seen a hook for a while. I climbed the last untouched hill with my daughter, while barn swallows swooped like little blue angels from nest holes in the cliff face. From the heights, I could see the church steeples of Three Rivers, and how cottonwood and sassafras saplings had reclaimed the bare ground below. I remembered too, with some regret, where I had dug and carried. Of how car-sized shelves of earth would fall from these cliffs as diesel-belching machines clawed it away.

Then, perhaps because the pit was now almost pastoral, I thought of my great-grandparents. Of the 700 apple, cherry, plum and peach trees they'd planted. Of how the whole family would strap on picking buckets and ride a hay wagon into the knobs to pick Red Delicious apples on Sunday afternoons in October. Of the rumble of apples as they filled bins in the barn, of my great-grandmother's apfelstrudel dough that she'd roll out across the entire dining room table. And finally, how their family legacy would one day vanish under the blade of a bulldozer.

It's not that I faulted my younger self for what came next. I'd been a teenage serf, the smallest of cogs in an earth-eating machine that I neither owned nor understood. But still. I was part Mayer, and our kin didn't come here to violate and destroy, to ruin and obliterate the fair hills of the Lord. We love trees, apples, gardens and rivers and spend our best days close to them. What a travesty that nothing they built has remained.

I walked south across the hills, searching for a lost remnant of the Mayer orchard. Not a single old apple tree did I find. Only a thorny tangle of multiflora rose, which grew like the spiteful curse of an aggrieved god. But the outing did inspire me to learn more about the family's origins. I'd seen the stiffly posed black and white photos and heard snippets of oft retold stories. The larger context, however, was missing. We knew next to nothing about John and Marianna's native place — and how it formed them for what came next.

The one thing I did not want to explore in detail, however, was the family tree. As big a deal as Heldwig von Mayer may have been in 1723, his progeny wasn't my first concern. It was the lived-experience and history of their time and place I was after. What interested me most was a throwaway line I'd often heard from my grandmother. She left Cseb at age four, but somehow this much stayed with her: "We could hear the Danube from our window."

Hear the *Danube*? That would've made Cseb a river town.

Did this mean they were river people? Did they fish with long rods and floppy hats for pike and burbot? It was high time I knew more, and within 10 minutes — thanks to online research that would have taken my mother months to unearth — I had answers. Complete with demographic data and Instagram photos.

The mighty Danube does indeed flow past Cseb (aka Čelarevo) on its 1,770-mile course from the Black Forest of Germany to the Black Sea of Romania. So yes, my ancestors did move from one river town to another. Did those Balkan waters of memory dance in their veins when they came here? They would've known the riparian breezes, the humidity, the reflected light and fishy effusions that make Čelarevo feel like Three Rivers. John's shoe shop in downtown Three Rivers was a stone's throw from where the Portage and Rocky rivers join the larger St. Joseph. If he couldn't hear the St. Joe, he could sure smell it from there.

While Čelarevo sits on the 45th parallel, and Three Rivers on the 42nd, the average precipitation and seasonal temperatures for both are about the same. Photos of modern-day Čelarevo (pop. 5,550) show a village of brick homes, nestled in a tree-lined grid of streets that's not unlike Three Rivers. From Google Earth, you can see that residents have immense gardens, long rectangles behind their houses that abound with fruit trees, pole beans and cabbages. At the town's edge, the streets give way to the luxuriant green cropland of the Danube Plain.

Just as Čelarevo knows rivers, so does it know horticulture

and beer. It's home to the 1,235-acre Delta Agrar orchard, the largest of its kind in Serbia. Along with Delta Agrar, the other big Čelarevo employer is the Carlsberg Serbia brewery. They make LAV pale ale, one of Serbia's top brands. Carlsberg also sponsors the Serbian national football team and built a stadium for them on the edge of town. No signs of a Mayer family skybox, though.

For those fond of travelogue spiels, here's a few details about the high-tech Delta Agrar orchard. Its new cold storage unit can keep 20,000 tons of apples fresh for nearly one year. It does so by gradually adjusting the temperature and humidity levels as the apples ripen. They mainly grow Red Delicious, Golden Delicious and Granny Smith (I'd hoped for something more *Serbian*) but here's their angle. They raise their own trees, which have almost no side branches. The trees grow almost entirely vertical, like short, stout flagpoles studded with apples. Given their upright form, the trees can be planted 2.5 feet apart — instead of the usual 10 or 15 feet — and this efficient use of space has made their per-acre yield skyrocket.

Beyond the ag-gizmo stuff, it's the alluvial soils and moderating climate of the Danube River that matter most. These favorable conditions, much like the "terroir" of fine wine country, produce apples of rare sweetness and flavor.

Given their homeland's provenance, John and Marianna must have known something about orchards when they came here. Why else would cash-strapped shoemakers plant 700 fruit trees? When they saw the knobs, they must have felt in their bones that this was good apple country. They would have noted the well-drained soil and timely rains, the up and down-hill "air drainage" to fend off killing frosts, the cool autumn nights that ripened apples to peak sugar content. In this distant, yet familiar land, they could envision their Old Country dreams anew.

But as a point of fact, it was mainly Marianna who made it so. John worked days at his shoe shop and farmed in the evening. It was Marianna's drive and muscle that cleared 20 acres for the orchard and two acres for a vegetable garden that fed the family. It was Homeric toil, done in an age before rototillers, always with an eye and ear cocked toward the house where a bawling baby might need nursing. Yet in this decades-long pursuit, she was no peasant drudge or meek house frau. With a landscape architect's eye, she built sprawling flower beds, an ornamental goldfish pond, a circular drive enclosed by a scalloped hedge. Her home's beauty became a local landmark and minor tourist attraction.

Until the day when John came home early from work.

"Oh, Ma!" he said, and at age 74, collapsed and died in Marianna's arms.

From there, the House of Mayer faced rapid decline. On the advice of a relative, Marianna sold the family home for a song in what my grandfather always thought was a shady business deal. The new owner, who was no apple man, couldn't tear the orchard out fast enough. It was all that stood between him and the precious gravel below. Although Marianna moved just a few miles away, she never visited her home again.

She didn't want to taint her good memories with the barren ugliness that followed.

As for me, the climax of my time at the knobs wasn't as tragic — but it was memorable. My career dead-ended one day at 4:30 p.m. when a dump truck rolled into the pit for some gravel. It was past quitting time, and the equipment operators were already tipping cold cans of Bud in the garage. (And chain-smoking Marlboros. This was the '70s, no one got hysterical about honest vices). I didn't know how to drive the big yellow Case loader, but they were off the clock and told me to do it myself. It was terrible advice for a mechanically inept 17-year-old. I climbed into the high cab, got confused by all the levers and chaos soon followed. In a panic, I tore off the dump truck's tail gate. It dangled there from a bent lug bolt like a giant wind chime.

Well, the operators sure got off their lazy asses to come outside and see *that*. But never again would Jim DeBoer trust me with anything more dangerous than a shovel. Can't say that I blamed him.

So, here we are. What's left of the knobs may be protected, but the Mayer legacy has been lost to the ages.

Or has it? Because I choose to believe that some of the spores from Coon Hollow Road have taken root elsewhere. For 25 and 35 years respectively, my brother and I have tilled and planted. Our properties have hundreds of shade and fruit trees, a maze of hand-laid rock walls, a restored prairie, hives of honeybees, flocks of chickens and turkeys, and various sheep, goats and donkeys. They live in well-kept barns and graze land that was barren when we moved here. As did our Mayer forebears, we espouse our fealty to local apples, good beer and the papist view of our place in the cosmos. Maybe there's more to genetic traits and lineage than I thought.

Meanwhile, the pit stands as a workable compromise, the demilitarized zone of a cease-fire between man and nature. Would it be great to see someone plant another orchard on the remaining knobs? Of course. Yet for now, with the gravel played out, play of a gentler sort begins. Even if I can't quite fathom the idea of purple yoga tights in Jim DeBoer's truck garage. It would be good to tip a few Carlsbergs by the pond and think about that for a while.

From Dogs to Fur Babies — and Back Again

From a distance, you couldn't be sure of anything except that it was flat. All we knew was that for several days, our black lab, Melody, had dragged around a carcass of unknown origin. She'd throw it gleefully in the air like a rancid bouquet tossed by the bride at a zombie wedding. Then she'd shake it with mock fury and roll headlong until its crusty residue perfumed her neck and collar.

This was early spring, and not until Saturday afternoon, when she left it on the porch, did I realize the tattered thing's true identity. Given its ruddy color, I'd assumed it was the flattened remains of a squirrel. Yet from one intact corner there protruded a pussy willow-soft tuft of paw. From another sprouted a delicate spray of wiry white whiskers; clearly, the deceased had been of feline origin.

We dubbed it Flat Cat, and for the next two weeks the dog and her gamey chew toy were inseparable. It was Mel-Mel's habit to run out and greet my car as it pulled into the driveway after work. With Flat Cat's arrival, this endearing routine took on a new twist.

"Where's Flat Cat? Where'd she go?" I'd ask, in the inane, sing-song voice that adults reserve for dogs and babies. "Go get Flat Cat! Go get her!"

Mel-Mel would dash off, retrieve Flat Cat from the side yard and repeat her toss-and-roll maneuver. After several days of such rough use, it began to look less like an ex-cat and more like a mangy loincloth for a small caveman. Eventually, Flat Cat disappeared altogether, which likely meant that it was eaten in its crunchy entirety.

It's reasonable to ask why a person would stand idly by while their dog did such a dreadful thing. Relatedly, you could ask if a person would let their dog eat a dead coyote; browse on the spoils of a compost pile; unearth a recently buried and much beloved family cat; and eat a baby rabbit that's just been dug, still squeaking and writhing, from its grassy burrow.

If a person answers "yes" to these questions (as I can to all of them) then chances are they've got a country dog. Or at least a city dog that lives by country dog rules. By that, I mean a Paleo dog that's left as free as possible to pursue its true doggish nature. A country dog enjoys plenty of freedom with all the adventure and hardship that a life lived out-of-doors entails. It's a dog that's cared for, with ample food, water, shelter, and vaccines — but unless sick, is never pampered. It's a dog that might not live as long as its indoor brethren, but one whose life is infinitely richer in musky pleasures. Most

105

important, it's a dog that's never treated like, or expected to act like, a four-legged human being. A country dog is all that a "fur baby" is not.

Country dogs are an artifact of a less urban, less rulebound America. But paradoxically, while city dogs enjoy more doggy parks, doggy play dates and dog-friendly shops and stores, their elevated status burdens them with human constraints. Rarely, if ever, are city dogs free to hunt, procreate, roam nose-to-the ground off-leash, or relieve themselves privately. At least not without some hovering human who waits to pounce on their still-warm discharge with a dismal little plastic poop bag.

It wasn't always so. As recently as the 1970s or '80s, dogs occupied a lower rung on the social ladder. Even in town, they might live in a backyard doghouse where they chewed real bones and survived on table scraps or cheap canned pet food. They had dog names like Sport, Dixie, Buddy and Sarge. They were friendly enough, but your hand might smell a bit ripe after you petted one. Except for the rabies and distemper shots required by law, they rarely saw the inside of a vet's office. They would happily go years, as ours did, without a proper bath.

Today, millions of Americans have elevated their dogs to the status of life partner or surrogate child. In fact, single adults comprise the fastest growing segment of dog owners. In "One Nation Under Dog," Michael Schaffer writes that 85 percent of dog owners refer to themselves as the Mommy or Daddy of their canine. Forty-three percent of dog owners say their pet sleeps in bed with them at night. It's also telling that in 2018, all of the top 10 female dog names were of human origin: Bailey, Molly, Sadie, Lola, Daisy, Luna, etc.

Across the United States, spending on pets mushroomed from $15 billion in 1995 to $72 billion in 2018. We now have pet nutritionists, veterinary dermatologists, dog kennels with TVs, and — inevitably — lawyers who specialize in pet custody cases. The sad irony, animal experts say, is that dogs can get confused and misbehave if we treat them too much like people. They expect us to be leaders of the pack. Nonetheless, thousands of "pet parents" now medicate their animals for doggie ADD, anxiety, depression, and other human-like disorders.

But what if we're trying to make a simple, fur-bearing mammal serve a social purpose that it's genetically unsuited to fill? Further, what if it's not just *the dog* that needs therapy? As Edward Abbey said, "When a man's best friend is a dog, then that dog has a problem."

If that's true, then many of the 46 million U.S. households who own dogs would be guilty as charged. Like me, they consider their couch-surfing, human bed-sleeping, crochet-vested dogs as part of the family. Like me, they rely on their dog to give love and emotional support in ways that a self-absorbed spouse, partner, sibling, or distant child who rarely calls or visits does not. So, who cares if Angel and Pretty Boy never leave their 100-square-foot patch of yard or synthetic grass? Do I expect them to tree mountain lions or rundown meth dealers? No, but I hope that some dogs will, if given the opportunity. Just as I hope that some wolves will always run free to hunt elk at Yellowstone.

There's more here to say about the virtues of good country dogs, but first let me offer two caveats. For starters, letting a dog enjoy country-style freedom still requires — dare I say it — plenty of active "parenting" on your part. Country is not a synonym for feral. This isn't about making your home a fortress of anarchy where slavering Rottweilers keep animal control officers at bay. If you and your dogs are that unhinged, rural Alaska would be a better place to unleash your "Revenant" inclinations.

Further, neither does country dog status excuse an owner from the usual demands of pet care. If anything, an outdoor dog may require more attention than a zirconia-bedazzled Fur Baby. This could include bedding straw, a freeze-proof water bowl, a heat lamp or rabies booster shot should Beaux-Beaux go a few rounds with a skunk or raccoon. Yet it's good medicine for both of you. Mel-Mel gets me off my arse each night because no matter if it's 90 above or 20 below, she simply *must* *sleep* in the barn. She'll whine and paw until, with a deep, existential sigh, I rise from book and chair for the 150-foot gangplank walk to her cement-floored stall. Once back inside, a warm house never felt so good.

If you think this all sounds unnecessary, or like a nostalgic attempt to restore America's lost Lassie-hood, then I would agree. By and large, country dogs are unnecessary to the way most of us live now. However, just as some men don scratchy wool uniforms of blue and gray, and pretend to kill each other in mock combat on Civil War battlefields, so do I choose to retain a semblance of the bond that's existed between people and dogs for 15,000 years running.

Most of us know, if only from TV pet food commercials, that wolves are the ancestors of modern dogs. Exactly how humans and dogs became such close partners remains a point of dispute. Some researchers claim that humans adopted wolf pups and raised them as pets. Others, such as Brian Hare from Duke University, believe it was the wolves that approached us first. In primitive times, wolves would scavenge around garbage dumps on the edge of human settlements. According to Hare, those that were bold and aggressive were killed, while those that were bold and friendly were welcome. And not only for platonic reasons. During times of famine, the archeological digs show that dogs were often eaten as emergency food rations. Even today, many cultures still regard Fido as a viable entree. The South China Morning Post reports that 80 percent of Vietnamese regularly eat dog meat, as do 20 percent of Chinese and 60 percent of South Koreans.

Over time, Hare writes, the dogs that early humans chose as companions began to look different than wolves. They grew floppy ears, splotchy coats and waggy tails, traits that made them look more friendly. Along the way — and this sealed the deal in terms of our mutual bond — dogs developed the ability to read human gestures. In fact, Hare writes, dogs are similar to human infants in how they pay attention to us. This trait made early dogs more trainable and well-suited for hunting. It also suits them for the only "work" that's required of most dogs today: providing emotional support for their owners and loved ones. This now extends to those earnest, middle-aged parents who buy "I ♥ My Grand Dog" bumper stickers.

In terms of today's country dogs, there are many useful breeds that still earn their keep around farms and ranches. But in my situation, it's been the sturdy, mild-mannered mutts that have fared best. The specialized breeds — a bluetick hound and border collie — proved hard to manage. It wasn't their fault. They were working dogs, bred for work that I couldn't give them. I had no raccoons to hunt, no sheep to herd across the nomadic plains. My four acres were too small, and their urge to roam too boundless, for them to thrive here.

With a good mutt, I'm able to raise a country dog with a homebody's heart. In practice, this means they learn the extent of their home ground and rarely stray from it. It's where they're happiest. It's where they'll stick around to dig, wallow, and explore — even with no fence or shock collar to bind them there.

Not being a dog trainer, I can't exactly say how dogs and humans come to this agreement. Although much like raising human children, I suspect that it begins with the gift of being present. A dog's demeanor changes when they spend long hours outside with you, their beloved pack leader. They become less clingy, less likely to tear off in a manic fit like over-sugared kids turned loose at recess. Once unburdened of excess energy, they'll nose about while you tend a peaceable kingdom that man and beast can enjoy together. The vegetable garden and overgrown field. The fruit trees and raspberry brambles that provide food and cover for birds, squirrels, turkeys, rabbits, and woodchucks. With your company and some sniff-worthy habitat nearby, why should they stray anywhere else?

Gradually, a good country dog will strike a balance between companionship and shouting-distance accountability. They're not underfoot when you're in the garden or strawberry patch. They know enough to give a tractor or chainsaw the right of way. They'll chase your barn cat up a tree, but not mail trucks and kids on bikes. Then every so often, after you've split just enough firewood or weeded a long row of tomatoes, they'll sidle up and give an amiable "woof." Scratch them behind the ears and you'll both feel the better for it.

All this and more we stand to lose if we relegate the age-old ways of country dogs to the anthropological dust bin. If nothing else, we should keep some country dogs around as brood stock and reminders of how the first human/dog friendships came to be. Because we, as much as dogs, need to retain some vestige of wildness. Even when they kill little live things that we wish they hadn't or roll with joyful abandon in things that we find gag-inducing.

Remember, these are *dogs*. Must we micromanage their every instinct and pleasure? It's been about 150 centuries since dogs consented to live around the hearth with humans. In truth, they're no longer born to be wild. But whenever we can, it doesn't hurt to unhook the leash, cry havoc, and let them live that way.

The Bonfire of the Inanities

A science teacher will tell you that a fire requires three basic ingredients: fuel, oxygen and a source of ignition. But come spring in rural Michigan, there's a fourth essential ingredient: stupidity. A case in point being the two-acre, run-away brush fire that I ignited the first spring my wife and I moved into our farmhouse.

In my defense, the small fire that I meant to set was necessary. Anyone who lives in an old house on a few acres in the country ends up with a lot of woody material that's too expansive to haul away. In our case, the pile included not just the usual pruned limbs and fallen branches, but several pickup loads of wood scraps.

Delmont and Harriet, the Depression-era farm couple who owned the home and farm before we did, were by today's standards compulsively thrifty. They may not have saved everything, but they certainly saved everything worth saving. In the attic, for instance, we found *22* sawed-off broom handles.

112

It's not clear why. Did they foresee a day when the replaceable broom head would be invented? In the lean-to shed were two-dozen orphan screens and storm windows, along with several storm doors. None of them, it should be noted, fit a single door or window in the house.

All this and much more I heaped on a burn pile that was eight feet high and 10 feet across. The pile was in a one-acre field that was bound by a cornfield, a row of blue spruce and the mowed side yard that adjoins our home.

It was an overcast spring day, and while most of the pile seemed dry, I had a hard time getting the damp stuff at the bottom to ignite. It needed help. It needed what fire marshal types call an accelerant. For that purpose, one could reasonably use a few pages of dry, crumpled newspaper. Then in a flash, I was overcome by a reckless idea — the kind that usually gets curious 12-year-olds in big trouble.

"You know what?" I asked myself, as a devious tingle traversed my spine. "I bet that a jelly jar of gasoline would really make this baby take off!"

As a matter of fact, it did. What I hadn't expected was that the fire would talk to me. One second after the match was lit, in a most violent tone of voice, the fire clearly said "WOOOFFFF!" Within five seconds, it had morphed into an angry, malevolent being — a Great Fire Beast that was straining to burst its ankle chains. And by the time 10 seconds passed? Let's say that I finally understood what's meant by the term "exponential growth."

Exponential growth has become a throwaway phrase that

even non-math types like to use in casual conversation. As in, "If that happens, we'll see exponential growth in the XYZ industry." Well, do you want to see exponential growth defined? Do you want to see a force of nature increase by the square root of its size within a few seconds? Then do this. Dump a jelly jar of gasoline onto a pile of dried lumber scraps and dry leaves that's topped (forgot to mention this earlier) with a few hundred pounds of wrist-diameter pine branches. For dramatic effect, make sure the branches ooze resinous sap and bear a load of crunchy brown needles.

Within 30 seconds, the fire was unstoppable. More accurately, it was unstoppable with the paltry tools I had at hand. These being a yard rake and garden hose. The WOOOFFFF! became a ROAR-R-R-R! as the flames soared 10, 20, 30 feet into the air.

It was spring and there was dry grass in ready supply. Not short, green turf grass, but orchard grass. Brown and thickly matted, it hadn't been mowed, burned or grazed in 10 years or more. And the Fire Beast was hungry for it. With a savage crackle, it made a frightful leap and jumped *behind* me to form a perfect circle of fire around the burn pile.

Next, I did what any scared and remorseful 12-year-old would do in that situation. I ran to the house and screamed for Mommy to help.

"Nance, come out here, the fire took off and it's spread to the field!"

"Should I call the fire department?" she yelled back, in the shrill voice that wives reserve for such occasions.

"Uh, no. Let's not do that yet. They'll charge us $300 for the call. It's not that bad."

Actually, it was that bad. But pride got the best of me, as I have friends on the volunteer fire department who would never let me forget it. Instead, we fought the fire together, or rather tried. We dashed around with leaf rakes to beat the flames and tried to douse them with the meager spray of a garden hose. It was no use. We watched, helpless, as the fire spread under the blue spruce windbreak. It jumped to the next field in a rush of yellow-green flame.

It was our neighbor, Harry, a 70-something farmer, who saved the day. At first, I worried more about him than our property. Harry's a sturdy guy, but he's no fast mover. And now he shows up, as the fire rages on, armed with what? A flimsy hand-held garden sprayer? Chrome wand in hand (not much bigger than a band leader's baton), he strolls easy amid the flames. As if he's there to sprinkle Sevin dust on Japanese beetles that have troubled his wife's roses.

Incredibly, it works wonders. The fine spray, when directed at the base of the flames, snuffs them out cold. Ten minutes later, it's all over. The Fire Beast, like a slayed dragon, exudes a few feeble puffs of smoke and steam as its life ebbs into the charred stubble.

A bit sheepish, I ask "So Harry ... how did you know to come down?"

"Well," said Harry, in laconic, Midwestern-farmer fashion, "I saw the smoke from my house and figured you needed help."

What's politely implied here is that's he's lived in the coun-

115

try long enough to put two and two together. This is spring, the time when controlled burns often get out of hand. Further, he's got a new neighbor who obviously has no experience, and no business, trying to manage a grass fire. Unlike me, Harry's knowledge came from 60-plus years of farming. He didn't just read a two-page article in an organic gardening magazine.

Harry's gone now, but I've learned and applied what he taught me those many years ago. It's been an education in fire management, but also something deeper. It's made me see why such dimwit adventures, burnt wrist hair and all, are better for us than we know.

Because in fact, we don't have to burn anything. It doesn't take fire to keep the woody growth at bay in our little prairie. A tractor with a sturdy deck mower can easily reduce it to inch-high stubble. Yet what fun is that, I ask? Don't we already have enough machines to keep us at arm's length from the elemental forces of creation? We confine the beauty of brother fire to little steel boxes — furnace, boiler, oven, water heater. We dam the chaste currents of sister river to turn electric turbines, and entrust our drinking water supply to a dark Mordor of rusty pipes whose source and condition we scarcely know. Ask anyone in Flint.

If only in puny rebellion, can you blame an office drudge who wants to torch the grassy little moat around his castle now and then?

❋ Back When the Flames Ran Free

Before we set the next fire, it seemed prudent to further my knowledge of not only fire science, but local history. To misquote Santayana, those who forget history are doomed to get burned by it. As it turns out, I'm not the first pyro to inhabit the property.

The land's original tenants were the Potawatomi, who by all accounts were superb fire managers. They set fires to keep the native grasslands free from underbrush. The open space kept biting insects at bay and made it easier to hunt game and detect the approach of enemies. Centuries of such practices created a prairie and oak savanna landscape that early white settlers described as "park-like." Soon after, with all the panache and flair we've come to expect from edgy Midwesterners, they dubbed the place Park Township.

Most of these facts came from "St. Joseph County in Homespun," a local history published in 1931 by Sue Silliman of Three Rivers. It's well-researched and well-written, with none of the manifest destiny apologias we might expect from a white woman of Silliman's era. She fairly depicts how the local Indians were conned, threatened and otherwise screwed out of their land holdings. There's one thing missing, though. It's the one spectacular aspect of Native American life that I've never heard any historian describe. The mind-blowing, full-bodied adrenalin rush that must come when you torch a

117

55-square mile grassland like Prairie Ronde north of Three Rivers.

Can you imagine the unbridled freedom of it all? Probably not. We live in a society where people sue for millions should they be served a cup of too-hot cocoa at a fast-food restaurant. The Potawatomi, by contrast, were bound only by the social and religious customs of their clan and tribe. For matters such as a prairie fire, they'd let experience and reason be their guide.

The warriors, and maybe the women and kids too, would light their cattail torches and let 'er rip. They'd unleash the "red buffalo" and let it stampede across the grassy swells and swales of Prairie Ronde. And who knows? Maybe sometimes the fire escaped and burned all the way to hell-and-gone, clear into northern Indiana. It was theirs alone to control, theirs alone to reap the benefits or suffer the consequences. This was the world as they knew it, unbound by the hubris of invisible, straight-line boundaries. And we — we with our speed limits, city limits, credit card limits and Gordian knot of rules that grow every year more tangled and restrictive — we think *we're* free?

What would the first landlords of this place think of us now?

✹ *The Fire this Time*

Despite this laissez-faire precedent, our second prairie fire would have to be better planned and managed. We at least needed to learn the basic tools and tactics. For that, a manual by the Wisconsin DNR that showed how the big boys do it proved interesting reading.

As with 21st century everything, the once simple act of starting a grassfire has become dauntingly complex. For a 20- or 30-acre fire, the DNR used a crew of 15 firefighters and at least $1 million worth of equipment and vehicles. There was a burn boss, a burn plan and a burn permit. There were factors such as temperature, humidity, wind speed and wind direction to calculate. A photo showed the burn crew, in identical turnout gear, as they read a "prescribed burn document." That's something the Potawatomi would've carried around in their head!

On a homegrown fire, absent the G.I. Joe hardware and mesomorphic manpower, you need to improvise. This time around, I took the lawn tractor and mowed a four-foot wide path around the ½-acre we planned to burn. Not an impervious fire break, but much better than nothing. At intervals of 30-40 feet, I set five-gallon buckets of water — a poor man's fire extinguisher. A la Harry, there was a garden sprayer and some sturdy rakes and brooms to steer the fire away from places where it didn't belong.

But there'd still be that "I-really-shouldn't-do-this" tingle as I lit the first match. You can't engineer away all the danger and who'd want to? Like a surfer on a gnarly wave, the goal is to ride the crest but not get capsized.

True to form, the fire took off much faster than expected. (Controlled burn, while not exactly an oxymoron, is the most hopeful of phrases.) Then after it swept through 15 feet of orchard grass, the flames settled down and became easy to redirect.

Absent the histrionics, a grass fire becomes enjoyable to manage and observe. You can study how its size, shape, color and even sound varies based on fuel source. A clump of little blue stem grass flares and hisses briefly like a miniature firework. Woodier vegetation, like the stalks of tall coreopsis, make a hotter fire. The waxy leaves of black oak and dainty heads of Queen Anne's lace, cupped like hummingbird nests, each leave their own scent and signature of flame.

It was still a fire, but the earlier sense of uncontrolled violence was gone. Instead of a Fire Beast unchained, this one lapped about my feet and shins like a happy puppy.

As the flame front eased along, my wife's van pulled into the driveway. As I hoped, she came out to inspect the operation. "Well Nance, no fire trucks and no Harry — so far," I said. "And look at this (I raised a foot in the air) my boots aren't even smokin' yet!"

She gave a guarded smirk, the kind reserved for children who do something stupidly funny that you don't want to encourage. Then, to my surprise, she joined me on the fire line.

She still wore her lawyer's office work clothes, a well-dressed firebug in celery green sweater and robin's egg blue jacket. I've always thought that British nobles look foppish when they don ties and tweed for outdoor pursuits. Who wants a Windsor knot clutched at their throat as they fish a wild river for salmon? Yet on a buttery soft spring evening, to dress colorfully and well for a prairie burn seemed fitting. It brought to mind what a Hebrew psalmist wrote some 3,000 years ago: "Worship the Lord in holy attire." We were using an elemental, even sacramental life force to restore a patch of creation that had suffered from decades of ill use and neglect. Why dress like a slouch for such a regal undertaking?

Then, as if to complement my wife's fashion palate, the sky grew bifurcated as dusk gave way to dark. It took on the layered vibrancy of a Hopi sand painting. A rim of orange streaked the horizon before it faded to azure blue overhead. In the foreground, yellow flames danced against the black smudge of the scorched prairie. In the middle stood our farmhouse, its classic vertical form broken only by a rectangle of creamy light from the kitchen.

All gorgeous, but what is that plaintive sound? Is it the wail of a ... *distressed child*? Yes, our youngest daughter. With no shortage of volume, even 150 feet away, and her nose smashed flat to the window. She'd pulled away from the TV long enough to discover that her parents were outside. She wanted her mother *now*, and screamed something about, "Daddy burn the house down." Other pleas and threats ensued, until Mom relented and went inside to cook pasta.

❊ *Against the Wind, Softly*

By the time the stars came out, the work was over. There'd been a few flare-ups, but no risk to life and limb. We'd burned from west to east so the flames would hold into the easterly wind instead of run with it. "Against the Wind," as Bob Seger would have it. And as a former paratrooper, that's one principle I could understand. Believe me, you don't want to slam into the ground with 15 knots of wind at your back. It's better to turn your parachute into the wind — "knees to the breeze" — and drift down with as little forward movement as possible.

On this night, the fire also settled down nicely for a soft landing. At 9:30 p.m., sooty and well-spent, I snuffed out the last few embers and beelined to the kitchen for some warm garlic bread. On the way in, feeling triumphant, I made plans to burn an even bigger patch of prairie next year. I also wondered for the hundredth time if I couldn't someday make another parachute jump without busting up my right hip again.

Come morning, I knew that a burned field would greet the day and that the blackened earth would better absorb the quickening warmth of spring sun. With the detritus of seasons cleared away, the next rendition of blue-stemmed prairie could readily sprout to life.

Oddly enough, the fire also reminded me of my visits to Niagara Falls. As a child, and as an adult, the falls had given me the same sense of vertiginous longing. As I held the railing and watched tons of blue-green water thunder endlessly over black cliffs of doom, I felt a distinct urge to *jump*. It wasn't suicidal. It was simply that, for a few heady seconds, to slip the surly bonds of earth and leap headlong into roaring oblivion seemed like the ultimate expression of human freedom.

When confronted by the burning prairie, I felt a similar emotion. Whether it's waterfall or fire fall, the unyielding power of nature often treads the line between exhilaration and disaster. Unless your boots smoke a little, then maybe you haven't trod close enough.

A Life Indefatigably Lived

After a Memorial Day tornado tore through our neighborhood a few years ago, the skies had scarcely cleared when a chorus of chainsaws and generators echoed through the land. Just like that, my indefatigable brethren were out in force.

You'll find types like these scattered across the Upper and Lower Peninsulas. They're rough and ready men and women who'd just as soon wear Carhartt to their own weddings — and probably funerals. They drive professionally muddy pickups that bear the coveted "Log/Farm" Michigan license plates. They keep vintage tractors in their barns, stump-pulling brutes wrought from Eisenhower-era iron that stand oiled and primed for any emergency. When no one's around, I suspect they may even call them by lovey-dovey nicknames and whisper fondly into their single-barrel carburetors.

At Gerald's place down the road, a ghastly tangle of splintered maples covered his yard and driveway. It looked like a week's worth of cleanup. Yet a crew of indefatigables — they run in packs — had the whole mess buzzed up and hauled away by noon the next day. No mere funnel cloud can deter a steel-toed crew like that.

Since I've never trusted myself with a chainsaw, I had to show my defiance in a less defatigable fashion. I boldly went ahead with the cookout we'd planned for that evening. We grilled our beefalo burgers in a backyard littered with tornadic debris. Then we ate up all the potato salad, since I've never bought a generator for when the power goes out. The uprooted blue spruces — which hours earlier had shuddered and crashed to the ground as my daughter and I sprinted for cover in the barn — could wait.

And wait they did until well past the 4th of July ... of the next year. My brother-in-law Bob, himself a true indefatigable with a full inventory of countryman hardware, had to bail us out. He cut up the trees and yanked out the stumps with his John Deere tractor. Their orange roots quivered, twanged, then popped loose like the ganglia of a giant woody tumor.

We heaped dry branches around the big stumps and started an eyebrow scorching bonfire. While the branches soon burned to ash and cinders, the stumps were the same size as before. They smoldered on for three days and I puzzled about what to do. Leave them as primitive lawn art and ring them with marigolds? Encircle them with tractor-tire flower planters, (painted white) per the local fashion?

Then, when I finally nudged one of the stumps with my foot, I found that it was nearly as light as a Styrofoam stage prop.

It was a charcoal facade of its former self. All of its heft had burned and evaporated away. I could easily drag it by hand to a nearby field. Its presumed weight had a been a figment of my procrastination.

The stumps are an apt reminder of what happens when life (disguised as my old farmhouse) overwhelms you. It makes you over-estimate the difficulty of just about everything. You neglect to weed the flowerbeds, lately overrun with oak seedlings and poison ivy. The same goes for the leaky chimney flashing or the moldy couch "temporarily" stored in a dilapidated shed. Paralyzed by despair and self-pity you begin to ask, "How and when will I ever find time to do all this?"

Some of it never. I put off cleaning our dungeon-like Michigan basement for 19 years.

Yet in defense of fellow procrastinators everywhere, let me explain the well-intentioned thinking that makes it so. The procrastinator's problem isn't simply that he (I'll speak only for males) does too little. Rather, it's that he tries to do too much. When a procrastinator envisions "this weekend," he pictures a sunny interlude with unbound time to fish, garden, nap, hike, grill out and putty storm windows. That, instead of the scattered five or six free hours that he actually has to get something done.

Recently, I've read something about the steadfast work habits of writer John McPhee that should give any procrastinator inspiration. McPhee has published 29 books on subjects that range from oranges to canoes. This has made him one of the most prolific nonfiction writers of the 20th century.

Remarkably, though, he never writes more than one, single-spaced page a day.

"You know," McPhee says "you put an ounce in a bucket each day and you get a quart."

For this summer, I have vowed to master the art of the bite-sized project. There's no need to let the perfect (the mythical endless weekend) become the enemy of the good (a productive evening's work). In 45 minutes after supper, any reasonably fit human with a handsaw can prune a dozen dead branches off a blue spruce. Or fill two wheelbarrows with garden weeds. It's nothing profound, but it does assure tangible progress over the course of a week, month, season and hopefully, a life. We procrastinators — especially those who aspire to indefatigability — just need a swift kick in the bucket now and then to remind us of that.

GARDEN GREENS

TO SUPERIOR DREAMS

Turtle Savers of the World Unite

There's so much four-legged carnage along the roads of Michigan that it's easy to get jaded by the sight of it all. The rigor-mortised deer and eviscerated raccoon; the opossum that's no longer playing possum. They rush past at 60 or 70 mph like so many furry speed bumps, with only a self-interested crow or turkey vulture to officiate over their remains.

Not so the noble turtle. To see one slain seems especially sad and deeply unfair. I mean, it's a *turtle*, for God's sake. It can't dash, hop or change direction on a dime like an acrobatic squirrel can. No, a turtle's ponderous slog across the pavement most likely ends with disaster on the half-shell. There's either a nasty crunch or a carom shot that makes them spin off the road like a jettisoned hubcap. Some drivers even try to hit turtles rather than avoid them. In "The Grapes of Wrath,"

John Steinbeck devoted most of Chapter 3 to describe such a scene:

> *"... And now a light truck appeared, and as it came near, the driver saw the turtle and swerved to hit it (emphasis mine). His front wheel struck the edge of the shell, flipped the turtle like a tiddly-wink, spun it like a coin, and rolled it off the highway ..."*

Steinbeck pulled no punches in his fictional exposé of the Okie diaspora, with its labor-camp squalor and criminal inequality. But it's telling that this hard-shelled novelist couldn't bear to kill off the turtle, which in his account survives the collision.

Here in nonfiction land, it's been my experience that once a turtle gets whacked it's done for. Its wonderfully adapted shell, a lifelong home and fortress impervious to all predators, did not evolve to withstand the 3,000-pound footprint of an automobile. Yet until turtles as a species catch up, they'll no doubt continue their stoic, quixotic quest to cross two- and four-lane gauntlets of asphalt.

In a response that's no less quixotic I have started a new club to help them. It's called the Free and Self-Appointed Protectorate of Esteemed Turtle Savers. Anyone can join. There are no dues, no newsletter, no meetings, no administrative balderdash of any kind. As the omnipotent leader, I will remain a shadowy figure and could care less if you wear a green plastic helmet and/or a Styrofoam carapace and chartreuse thong as your official uniform. Because all that a Turtle Saver in good standing needs to do is this: stop and pick up a turtle whenever they see one do something fatally boneheaded, such as crossing a road or highway.

Then, carefully and *safely* (no need to make yourself roadkill) move the turtle to the other side. Be sure to carry it toward the direction it's already headed. Most turtles are driven by a strong maternal urge to build a nest or find a critical food source. They need to go their own way, and your fancy human logic won't convince them otherwise. For good measure, place the turtle at least 20 feet beyond the road shoulder so they're concealed by natural habitat.

Be extra careful when you move a snapping turtle. The first time you pick one up, you'll see why. With its long neck extended, a snapper's frightful jaws can reach about anywhere on its body. And fast. I grab them by the base of their tail, although carefully as to not damage any vertebra. Does my method give them a backache? Possibly, but not like an F-150 pickup will.

Once you've become alert to their plight, you'll find it's not only the big turtles that need saving. One day in late June, my daughter found a baby snapper in a roadside mud puddle. She named him Leonard, and for two weeks he lived in a tub on our front porch where he ate worms and lettuce. But a turtle deserves more from life than a Tupperware holding cell. We carried Leonard to a weedy, froggy irrigation pond about a half-mile away.

On the walk home, a farmer drove up in his four-wheeler

to investigate. We were, after all, trespassers on his property. These days, along with droughts and insect pests, farmers have to worry about thieves who strip electric cable from their irrigation systems and sell it for scrap.

"How you doin'?" he asked cautiously. It was part question, part Midwestern-succinct interrogation.

Once we explained our turtle rescue and release mission his lined face relaxed a bit. It didn't hurt that one of our party had blonde pigtails and a pink Snoopy t-shirt.

"Yeah, they're really on the move now," he said. "This morning we found a big ole snapper in the cornfield so we put *her* back in the pond, too."

Imagine that. Here was a hefty, haggard farmer probably in his mid-50s with 1,000 acres worth of reasons to do something else. I'm guessing he had hypertension and a heap of six-figure debt riding on this year's corn harvest. Yet somehow, he'd just added the title of Turtle Saver to his endless job description.

Why? Maybe it's because random acts of turtle rescue protect something within ourselves that's equally wild and worth saving. As modern humans, we already spend most of our lives in shells of our own making. Except that ours, with their GPS, climate control and tinted windows (and that includes farm tractors), tend to insulate and alienate us from the plight of other beings.

Not so when we stop the car and get out to save a turtle from an almost certain death. Something about their plodding dignity elicits within us a fine sense of brotherly and sisterly care.

In a rare act of inter-species solidarity, we take off the armor of mechanical invincibility and put on the naked vulnerability of the flesh. The cars whiz by, often frightfully near, but our empathy emboldens us to virtuous action.

Although for me, I must confess to a less sanguine motivation. I save turtles out of no small need for redemption. It involves a memory that, after an otherwise happy life on the rivers of southwest Michigan, grieves me to this day.

It happened during my mid-20s, when I met a friend in the National Guard who impressed me with his military acumen and overall worldliness. I'd served in the military only as a weekend warrior, while he'd been on active duty for three years after high school. My adventures were limited to purple smoke grenades and peacetime Army bases. He'd been a Marine who saw combat against the Druze militia in Lebanon. His knowledge of all things martial (not to mention female) was in every way superior to mine.

"Roger" wasn't a hunter or fisherman. But he did enjoy the rigor of outdoor pursuits, so I invited him to canoe and camp overnight with me on my favorite stretch of the Portage River. It was a gorgeous late summer day, warm enough for shorts, yet with low humidity that foreshadowed the coming autumn. I'd brought a spinning rod because I planned to catch enough bass for a shore dinner of pan-fried filets. Roger's recreational tool of choice was a 9 mm Beretta handgun, which didn't surprise or trouble me at first. Our campsite was well off the road and I figured we'd plink a few cans for target practice.

We hadn't been on the water for 10 minutes before Roger's

true purpose, and true colors, became evident. I was in the aft, trying to steer with one hand and cast with the other. Then suddenly, in a great profanation of the river's solitude, a minor Armageddon broke loose.

BLAM, BLAM, BLAM … BLAM, BLAM, BLAM … BLAM, BLAM, BLAM.

"Roger, what are you … what the hell are you *shooting* at?"

I thought he may have dropped a beer can in the current so he could hit a moving target. Instead, his targets were living turtles. Painted turtles, mainly, their olive-green shells shiny, bright and innocent as they sunned on the bleached bones of deadfalls that rose from the water. Crack shot that Roger was, most of his rounds hit their target. (He'd earned the Army's expert rifleman badge, the one with oak wreaths. While I, myopic and shaky of trigger finger, could only manage a marksman's cross).

Some of the doomed turtles plopped off to sink in the muddy shallows. Others spun crookedly and sickeningly downstream. They oozed contrails of crimson, reminiscent of the smoke trails left by faltering bombers hit by flak over World War II Germany.

Lord have mercy, Christ have mercy. Not to mention Saint Francis, Wendell Berry and Aldo Leopold.

When Roger finally looked back at me (he had to stop and reload) he didn't say anything. But the grin on his face did. It wasn't cruel or diabolical; the look of someone who found joy in evil. Instead, and this was nearly as bad, it registered no awareness of the beastly thing he'd just done for sport.

To say the least, it was an ugly revelation. He was *Roger.* He was the smart, funny, capable guy who men wanted to befriend and who girls couldn't resist. Now, as a guest on my beloved river, he'd revealed a cold-blooded apathy of a sort I'd never encountered. Of all the worldly things that he knew and that I didn't, how could he not know this?

No one had ever explicitly told me "Thou shalt not wantonly kill animals for the fun of it." I knew it, all the same, from a father who made us clean the fish we brought home, no matter how late, hungry, mosquito-bit or inclined we were to pitch a stringer of stiffened blue gills into the trash. I knew it from my friend's father, Mike, who was himself a lifelong turtle killer, albeit for subsistence purposes. He'd lure big snappers from the St. Joseph River into steel cages that he'd bait with rotten chicken livers. Then he'd butcher and eat them, as I did one day when I joined his family for dinner. (Though I did not find, as Mike did, that different parts of the snapper tasted variously of beef, pork, lamb or chicken. It was all muddy river water to me.)

Roger, raised as he was in the Chicago suburbs, had missed such instruction. For him the outdoors was a 360-degree shooting gallery. Everything that moved was a pop-up target. As proof, by late afternoon he'd left dozens of dead turtles to rot in the clear waters of the Portage.

"Hey, haven't you done enough damage for the day?" I asked weakly, after he'd blasted the first four or five. "What did these turtles ever do to you?"

"You know," I tried again, appealing to Roger's recent interest in things fashionably Taoist, "this is going to offend the great turtle consciousness. You're going to have bad some karmic debt to work out after this."

None of which had any effect whatsoever.

There are sins of commission and omission, what we have done and what we have failed to do. And I had failed on both counts. I should've stopped Roger and not just for the turtle's sake. Whether it's tax fraud, drunk driving, infidelity, drug use, workplace theft or wild game violations, the same principle holds. If we can't help friends see the error of their ways (and accept the same from them), then we defer the consequences to cops, juries, the IRS, homicidal spouses and even the Almighty himself. Each will settle the score in their own fashion.

It might have made all the difference if I'd simply said, "Roger, that's *enough* already. No more dead turtles. It's creeping me out. Besides, if the DNR sees us, we'll both be in deep shit."

Instead, I did nothing and if that doesn't make me an accomplice then I don't know what does. That's why I've pledged to save turtles until my own legs are slow, scaly and wobbly.

I've lost track of Roger and haven't heard from him in probably 20 years. I do know that he moved to Atlanta, became a policeman and then got promoted to detective. I stopped to see him once on a business trip, long ago. He told ghastly tales about headless, bullet-ridden drug dealers stuffed into the trunks of abandoned cars. Did blasting those turtles help prepare him for this? The cynic in me says that only a person inured to violence could survive a long career in big city law enforcement.

I also heard that Roger had started a family, and for all his mercenary bluster, that doesn't surprise me. He always had a soft spot for his young nephews. People do change with age and having kids can change us more than anything. So, who knows? The clogged roads of suburban Atlanta must surely imperil a host of wayward turtles. With a child onboard, maybe even a hard-shelled gunslinger could stop, get out and do right by the little live things in his care. At least I pray that it's so. A host of creatures, large and small, await his redemption.

Gut-Checked:
The Natural Redemption
of Lisa Rose

In the best photo I've seen of the photogenic Lisa Rose Starner, she picks hawthorn fruit from an unkempt tree entangled by a garland of wild grape vine. The setting is an early 21st century meadow near her home in suburban Grand Rapids, Michigan. But if it were a hawthorn bocage in 16th century Normandy, she would scarcely look out of place.

Lisa Rose appears in profile, her picking hand ablur with motion, her left hand cupped to receive the acorn-sized haws. Her unadorned hair, streaked blonde by summer sun, falls upon her shoulders. Her eyes gaze up at the harvest, as intently as one receiving communion in the hand. It's a timeless image, as befits the ancient trade of an herbalist.

Then there's the real life, as opposed to still life, version of Lisa Rose. It's the one at my elbow as we reconnoiter our little woods on the Portage River to hunt for wild edibles and medicinal plants. I'd signed up to attend her foraging workshop at a park in Grand Rapids but got the date wrong and missed it. She generously offered to drive 60 miles and repeat the class on my home ground.

There was also an ulterior motive, as I wanted to hear more about her big career change. For this was no mainstream transition from, say, human resources to predatory investment banking. No. Hers was a bodacious move — she'd traded a high-profile job in nonprofit management for this. Hers was now a life spent afield, immersed each day and season in nature's glory, free at last from bloviated meetings and office inanity. People paid her to identify plants that could dilate, purge, sedate, lubricate or inebriate them. What did it take to pull off a move like this? Lisa Rose made it all sound so effortless. At least until I learned of the hidden costs and requisite trials she'd suffered along the way.

The day she came to Three Rivers, the first plant we came across was mullein. It's an exotic from Asia and Europe, a tall spiky thing with little yellow flowers that I've seen grow five feet tall in old fields. To establish my woods cred, I repeated what I've heard naturalists say about the mullein's soft, fuzzy leaves. That they can be used as "Indian toilet paper."

"Eek! Don't ever use *that* for T.P!" she shrieked. "See those little hairs on the leaf? Those are like *fiberglass*. They'll really irritate your mucous membranes back there!"

The phantom itch that arose from my posterior told me that this advice alone was worth the $25 registration fee. Yet Lisa

Rose wasn't through with mullein. She was, in fact, effusive about its benefits when imbibed at the body's other end.

"Mullein is what's known as a 'cool plant,'" she said. "It's a diuretic; a 'quicker-picker-upper.' It clears water from tissues, such as the swelled joints that cause bursitis. It helps runners with IT band issues. (The iliotibial band runs along the outer thigh and knee. Lisa Rose runs marathons, so she should know).

"Mullein's also a relaxant, but it's not terribly sedative. You can make tea from the dried leaves. But run it through a coffee filter first or the hairs will make you *hack!*"

Here, she made a cat-with-a-hairball sound to underscore her point. It was very Lisa Rose: informative, entertaining, plant-nerdy and not what we'd expect from an herbalist.

The few herbalists I'd met were unreconstructed hippy chicks of the blowsy and frowzy variety. They were capable and congenial, but in their tie-dyed dotage had gone a bit mumbly-wizard inscrutable. Not so the omnivorous Lisa Rose. Think Heidi of the Alps, braids and all, with an MPA in nonprofit management and a BA in anthropology and French. With her, it's never just about plants. Her running narrative may veer into sociology, economics, medieval history, nutrition, federal drug policy or the fine-tuned proclivities of her eco-foodie palate. This is a woman who makes wild huckleberry margaritas. All the while, she talks to plants as if they were diminutive relatives well met at a family reunion.

"Oh my gosh, look at the *vaccinium!* They're so cute!" she

says, hailing the wild blueberries by their Latin genus. "Did you know there's 25 varieties of these? Their fruits are an antioxidant and their leaves are very astringent."

I did know some of that. Yet as Lisa Rose made clear, for an herbalist, plant identification is only half of the equation.

"You've got to know the 'energetics' of a plant and match it to the person's condition. Is a plant hot, dry, cold or damp? How does it work in the body? An herbalist has to orchestrate and formulate that. It's like knowing the right combination of people to invite to a cocktail party."

A case in point would be the marshmallow root tea that Lisa Rose gives her friend to sooth her professional singing voice. Or it could be whatever discomfited soul will need the pink-purple flower that we stumbled upon next.

"Hi guys!" Lisa Rose says, on her knees in the leaves to celebrate a cluster of wild geraniums. Among its uses, she says the astringent plant can be cooked in milk (at below 170 degrees) to treat diarrhea. It's a cure for that stretched out feeling that anyone who's suffered from a case of the runs knows too well.

"During an illness, our tissue can get prolapsed. It looks like a stretched-out balloon," Lisa Rose said. Her fingers traced a deflated balloon in the air. "Astringent herbs will tone and restore tissue to its original shape."

More talk on sassafras and stinging nettles followed as we toured the rustic apothecary of an oak hickory forest.

My favorite of these is the sassafras tree because its root beer fragrance reminds me of outdoor walks with my father. It's also mucilaginous, a word that's as slimy as it sounds.

It refers to the slippery ooze that sassafras produces when you chew on a twig or leaf. When swallowed, this mucilage helps coat and sooth inflammation of the stomach and intestine. Teas from aromatics such as sassafras, peppermint and spearmint also stimulate the production of digestive juices.

In describing the effects of wild plants on the body, one word that Lisa Rose came back to often was "gut." At first, it was jarring. It's a harsh word, gut, one that sounds, well, *guttural*. It has a consonant edge that we reserve for the hard truths of life. As in, "Why didn't you have the guts to tell me that face to face?" Or "My gut tells me that I really shouldn't take that job." Gut speaks of something both intuitive and visceral.

It's the latter sense that herbalists use to describe the benefits of plants to people. Their working definition of gut entails (entrails?) the lower gastrointestinal tract. It's the 25 feet of upper and lower intestinal tubing that extends downstream from the stomach to the anus. In a healthy person, the gut should be a place of microbial harmony. It is where supple intestinal organs work in salubrious fashion to move the good food we've eaten to a proper, easy exit.

Instead, the gut has become for many adults a dark and diseased battleground. A surfeit of sugary, fatty and low-fiber foods — made worse by too much stress and caffeine, and too little sleep and exercise — can throw our gut flora out of whack. Overuse of alcohol and drugs such as aspirin and ibuprofen can break down the intestinal lining. Taken together, these factors can cause irritable bowel syndrome (IBS), a painful and socially debilitating chronic disorder with no known cure. The symptoms include abdominal pain, cramping, bloating, and both constipation and diarrhea. IBS afflicts one in five Americans.

This number includes at least one herbalist by the name of Lisa Rose. Although in her case, this ailment has come with a silver lining. It was a gut check over IBS that led Lisa Rose to steer her life and career in a wilder, more soulful direction.

❈ Trapped in the "IBS Culture"

When I first met the "old" Lisa Rose in 2007, she was at the pinnacle of success — and on the brink of a painful setback. She didn't see it coming, but Type A personalities rarely do.

By mainstream standards, Lisa Rose was killing it. She was executive director of a popular and growing nonprofit known as Mixed Greens. She had a comfortable home, with a supportive husband and two healthy kids. She seemed to have the brains and energy of two or three average mortals. Seventy-hour weeks were common, with more work always on the way.

Her Mixed Greens staff built raised bed gardens at inner-city schools to teach kids about plants, nutrition, cooking and composting. Several neighborhoods they served met the USDA definition of a food desert. They had no grocery within a one-mile radius that sold fresh produce. When these children tasted blueberries or asparagus, it was often for the first time.

It all made for a great story. At one school, after someone dug up and stole the newly planted fruit trees, the students turned the tables. They wrote letters to the Grand Rapids Press that decried the vandalism. The public outcry led to increased support for Mixed Greens. Their media savvy and wholesome appeal (who can really be *against* a school garden?) made Mixed Greens, and thereby Lisa Rose, a rising star.

Alas, the world would not let such good deeds go unpunished.

In 2007, Mixed Greens' heady success led its' board and leaders to commit a textbook case of overreach. They agreed to merge Mixed Greens with the popular, but financially struggling Blandford Nature Center. The center, once owned by the Grand Rapids Public Schools, had been converted into a nonprofit organization. Mixed Greens was expected to take the helm and lead them to solvency.

Within 90 days, Lisa Rose knew this was a fool's errand. The Mixed Greens' business model was based on single classrooms and 6 x 6-foot raised bed gardens. It wasn't meant for a 143-acre nature center, with its grounds, buildings and maintenance headaches. The combined workload was too big and the budget too small. Lisa Rose had to "fire people that she didn't want to fire." It was a classic case of the minnow that swallowed the whale — and it left the head minnow with a seething gut ache.

"It was crazy," she said. "Here I am, trying to sell sustainability, and I'm so stressed out that my digestion has shut down. I was living the IBS culture and paying for it. I didn't even have time to sit down for a meal. All I could do was gulp a green smoothie on the way to work."

There's far more to the story, but here's the gist of it. After Lisa Rose helped Blandford raise grant money to ease the transition, she stepped down and let someone else run the show. Along the way, her beloved Mixed Greens became collateral damage and had to close up shop.

I had lunch with Lisa Rose at a Battle Creek brewpub shortly after the ordeal ended. She looked gaunt, visibly spent in mind, body and spirit. Life had just given her an ass-kicking of the sort that it reserves for the young and invincible. She wasn't broken, but she was sorely bent. Nonetheless, it was in that bending that she would find her redemption and renewal. Because when Lisa Rose bends over anywhere for long, she sees what most of us do not: the beauty and utility of wild growing things.

❋ *Regroup and Renewal*

Flip the calendar pages ahead five years and I'm standing on the balcony of her Grand Rapids home, which overlooks a wooded ravine. I point to a graceful tulip poplar whose limb brushes the railing. As usual, Lisa Rose can't help herself. Whatever wild plant she sees next becomes her favorite: "Oh, *Liriodendron*, the twig tips and flowers make an *amazing* spicy tincture. It macerates over time, and it makes excellent bitters for indigestion ..." etc., etc.

I had come to hear about Lisa Rose's new herbal enterprise and to meet her husband, Seth. Come to find out, instead of one job she now had about seven: herbalist, forager, author, naturalist, local food advocate, blogger and host of a cooking segment on local TV. She also called herself a "wild crafter." I wasn't sure if that was a separate job or all of the above.

What Lisa Rose had done was instructive for anyone who wants to rebuild their psyche and/or career. I wouldn't say she re-created herself — only the Creator can do that. But she did take her shattered pieces and potsherds and reshape them into a new and serviceable whole.

It helped that there was much good material with which to work. She was raised by a single mother in Spring Lake, Michigan, a village within earshot of the Lake Michigan surf. Nature was always close at hand — and mouth. Her mom canned and foraged her way through the Fruit Belt year because it was the cheap thing, not the chic thing, to do. Peaches, wax beans, Concord grape juice and morel mushrooms. They were food rich, but cash poor. Eating out at McDonald's was considered a "treat."

At Grand Valley State University, Lisa Rose started out as a music major but switched to anthropology. It was a fortuitous move. Anthropology taught her to see the layers and connections among people, culture and the natural world. Anthropology studies took her to France, where she focused on Neolithic agriculture (c'est what?) and learned the lore and medieval uses of Eurasian plants.

After college, Lisa Rose moved to California where she worked and volunteered in the Bay Area. She was mentored by Alice Waters, founder of the legendary Chez Panisse restaurant in Berkeley and éminence grise of the locally grown and edible schoolyard movements. For finishing school, Lisa Rose moved back to Michigan and "did grunt work" on an organic farm near Petoskey.

From there, a girl raised on government cheese would marry an Amway executive, start a hotshot, if star-crossed organization, and then chuck it all to gather wild plants for a living. Gone were the days, though, when Lisa Rose could trade on the prestige of a mainstream job title. The Chamber of Commerce was less interested once she put herbalist/forager after her name. An herbalist, especially in a conservative place like Grand Rapids, operates on the margins of social convention. She became like the shaman's hut on the edge of town, where the medically forlorn came for potions after all else has failed them.

"As a first option, people won't usually call some random plant lady who tells them to eat weeds," she said. "By the time people turn to me, they've tried 150 things and most of them haven't worked."

❋ Herbalism, from Soup to Nuts

Eating weeds … if only it were that simple. By law, an herbalist operates in something of a health care no-man's land. Per FDA regulations, Lisa Rose must preface her counseling with this disclaimer: "I am not a medical doctor, and cannot treat, diagnose or cure any illness or disease by law." It's how the government seeks to limit the quackery that still bedevils the unregulated field of alternative medicine.

Although in her practice, Lisa Rose takes a holistic approach that transcends herbal medicine.

"I'm not always about handing someone an herb. It all starts with listening to the patient. I had one client who was a hard-working, Type-A high achiever. She was super-stressed and reached the point where she was taking narcotics for insomnia. She wanted to lose weight and we started talking about her diet and herbs that could curb appetite."

Here, a profit-driven herbalist could've pitched some remedies to help the patient sleep more and eat less. Lisa Rose did not do so. She did pick up on how the woman kept returning to her past avocation as a competitive swimmer.

"Her eyes would light up when she talked about swimming. She thought she'd outgrown it, but you could see that it'd been her true joy. She'd worked hard in her career and had lots of stuff, but it didn't bring her bliss. We came to realize that what she really needed was to start swimming again. When she did, she lost weight and went off her sleeping pills."

Then there was the case of the woeful married guy. His home was nearly in foreclosure, his torn meniscus required knee surgery, and his four children kept hounding him for a puppy.

"I listened for 10 minutes and realized that I couldn't do anything about these other things. But I did tell him to get a dog for therapy. Not a puppy, but an old dog that he could walk with slowly. He needed quiet companionship as much as exercise."

For a good herbalist, that's the warp and woof of it. See a doctor when you must but do for yourself what doctors and big pharma cannot. Make yourself some homemade chicken soup. Get more sleep when you feel a cold coming on so that your body can resist it without antibiotics. Look for little patches of wild plants in your neighborhood, heretofore unseen, that might play a serendipitous role in your life.

For Lisa Rose, it's not enough to treat symptoms. That's small tuber stuff. She wants us to become foragers, passable cooks and minor prophets of sustainability in our own right. She wants us to tap the dank, sweet wonders of the local biota, and thereby re-energize a society that's become as denatured as the cheesy fries at a shopping mall food court. She wants us to feel so at home in the wild nearby that we become "like a dog who goes outdoors and chews on something soothing when she needs it." It's this mindfulness she teaches in her workshops on foraging and cooking. It's this detail you'll find in her definitive "Midwest Foraging," which describes uses for 115 wild edibles, from burdock to wild peach.

In an age of outsourcing, Lisa Rose's practice is truly a soup (bone broth, nettles) to nuts (hickory, walnut, beech) operation. Her business model resembles a diversified, World War II-era family farm. Only instead of draft horses, pigs, cows and chickens, her crops are flowers, seeds, berries, buds, bark and roots. She grows or forages some 70 species of medicinal plants, the raw materials for her Burdock & Rose Apothecary business.

Rather incredibly, she concocts her medicines on a modest, four-burner stove just a few feet from her dining room table. When Lisa Rose cooks, the herbal bounty must surely steam, stew and off-gas with primordial potency. One can only imagine what a bestiary of smells her kitchen has imprinted on the olfactory memories of her children. When it comes to trigger aromas of childhood, I doubt that Mom's pot roast will hold a candle to her Dark Storm Bitters.

❋ *How Little Brown Bottles Earn Shelf Space*

We have a cluster of her medicines on the shelf above our kitchen sink. They were a gift from Lisa Rose, and frankly, one that was not first appreciated. "It's OK," I'd heard her say,

"I know my friends have cupboards full of my stuff that they'll never use."

We'd done the same until we were leaving for vacation and our daughter, Emily, had a stomachache. This, as we were about to depart on a 30-hour Amtrak train trip from Kalamazoo to Albuquerque. A bit desperate, I remembered the Elderberry Elixir. Its contents include elder flower, sage, thyme, Echinacea and boneset.

After a few fatherly imprecations — "the train won't stop often, and do you want to be sick the whole away"? — I convinced Emily to drink a tablespoon of elixir, mixed in a few ounces of warm water. I'm not sure what she had, but within 10 minutes, her symptoms lessened considerably.

Later, my wife came down with a stomach virus that had reduced her to an inert heap of misery on the couch. Ibuprofen and acetaminophen hadn't touched it.

"Do you want to try some Dark Storm Bitters?"

"Sure," she said weakly, from beneath a mound of purple blankets. "It can't make me feel any worse."

Twenty minutes later, without saying much, she got up and went out to the kitchen to do what she usually does in the kitchen. Not cured, mind you (the FDA can't have that) but acceptably functional. That's how the weird little brown bottles, their black rubber eyedroppers fragrant with herbal extract, have earned cabinet space.

There are, no doubt, over-the-counter medicines that could have the same effect. Moreover, the herbals co-exist on a shelf next to my Advil, chewable vitamin C and blood pressure meds. I'm not ready to trade the convenience and reliability of big pharma for a mug of herbal tea that leaves green flecks in my teeth.

The difference, though, is that I feel good about herbal medicines. They appeal to me in a way that white pills made in the automated sterility of a far-off factory cannot. They smell a bit like the musky spears of skunk cabbage that resurrect each spring from the cold muck of a Michigan marsh. They taste of dark mysteries, still untamed. They contain the life essence of species that I know deeply and love entirely: maple, blackberry, goldenrod, purple coneflower. They are seasonal notes excerpted from the hymnal of unbroken song that marks a country year in the Upper Midwest. To lump such physical and spiritual connections under the term placebo — i.e. a cure that makes us feel better because we want it to — doesn't begin to do them justice.

And what if herbals do build on our child-like faith in the power of wild plants to make us well? Given their healing powers, is it so unreasonable to believe that they were put here for our benefit?

When my father had an enlarged prostate, we bought him some herbal tablets made with extracts from the fruit of the saw palmetto (*Serenoa repens*). He was anxious at the time, fearful of the scourge that had claimed some of his friends. I'm not sure if the tablets worked, but something about them did. His symptoms lessened, and for whatever reason, he never developed prostate cancer.

No less important, the idea of saw palmetto as an agent of

wellness cheered him greatly. When we lived in Florida, he'd become fond of what the locals called palmetto scrub. It's the pine/oak savanna forest where the bushy little palmetto palm thrives. In the mid-1960s, there were rattlesnakes, turkeys, even bears and panthers in the pre-Disneyworld palmetto scrub of central Florida. My father hunted turkeys there only once, but his love for it remained.

What a blessing, then, that a wild fruit from his salad days in Florida could bring healing in his later years. Who wouldn't wish to be made well by a plant that grows in a favorite place? Such divine utility, at arm's length, foreshadows the bounties of the eternal paradise described in the book of Ezekiel (47:12).

"By the river on its bank, on one side and on the other, will grow all kinds of trees for food. Their leaves will not wither and their fruit will not fail. They will bear every month because their water flows from the sanctuary, and their fruit will be for food and their leaves for healing."

In a more prosaic way, a beatific natural vision runs through Lisa Rose's "Midwest Foraging." She knows it's there, has plumbed its substance, root and rhizome, and sorely wants us to do the same. It's even more believable coming from one who has herself tasted the poisoned fruits of a hectic, misaligned life.

❋ *Giving Natives Their Due*

As an armchair forager, I own several field guides on edible and medicinal plants. Lisa Rose's "Midwest Foraging" stands apart from similar books in two important ways.

The first is how it reflects her culinary training and cosmopolitan panache. Take currants. She says that the wild, purple berry "shines when served fresh over soft, local cheese." They also bake nicely, which makes currants well suited for berry tarts, breads and muffins (very Michigan), but also in pate de fruits and an "amazing classic French clafoutis pastry" (very Francophile, a la Lisa Rose). Elsewhere in the book, Lisa Rose elevates even the humble black walnut to Michelin-star status. Apparently, un-hulled green nuts can be "transformed" into a traditional Italian digestif (after-dinner drink) known as nocino.

The second big distinction with "Midwest Foraging" is how Lisa Rose approaches native foods on their own terms. She doesn't treat them as a replacement or filler for something else. That wasn't true in my Boy Scout days, when foraging guides gave us bowdlerized recipes that could've come from my mother's Betty Crocker cookbook. The implied, ethnocentric message was that natives couldn't be trusted in their natural state. To subdue already tender stalks of cattails, we'd boil them furiously in canned chicken broth or suffocate them in Campbell's Cream of Mushroom Soup. I can't say that I've tested the recipes in "Midwest Foraging." My cooking skills don't extend far beyond soup, chili and grilled campfire meats. But it's clear that Lisa Rose treats native foods as citizens of the world that can be incorporated — rather than subjugated — into prepared dishes from a range of traditions.

In her urbane knowledge of foods wrought from natives, Lisa Rose has eclipsed the pragmatism of her foraging mother. That's what precocious, blue-collar kids are driven to do. We claw our way to the degrees, jobs and acclaim that our parents were denied.

Inside, the chipped-cup folkways remain. Nocino and mojitos notwithstanding, Lisa Rose says her favorite wild plants, are "ditch weeds." The coarse and common Eurasian immigrants such as chicory, dandelion, burdock and purslane. They are a sign of foodie contradiction in an age when heirloom tomatoes sell for $3 per pound. Ditch weeds thrive in old fields, near shuttered factories and in the brushy margins of poor neighborhoods. Which doesn't deter Lisa Rose in the slightest: "I'm comfortable working in places that are rough."

That's the paradox for modern herbalists. They can take an unloved nuisance plant, one free for the picking, and convert it into a pricey curative that mainly appeals to a college-educated, middle-class clientele. As much as anything, this shows how the food economy that my grandparents knew has been turned on its head. For them, home remedies and local, organic produce were the affordable choices. Before World War II, nearly all produce was organic. It was the store-bought processed foods and medicines that cost more — and had consumer cachet.

Today, it's the cheaper processed foods, rife with salt, corn syrup and Frankenfood fillers, that are déclassé in the eyes of many consumers. That woman in faded overalls — with the master's degree in divinity and the rainbow do-rag — who brings her lumpy, organic apples to the farmer's market? What she's selling has become the fashionable, expensive stuff.

I saw this conundrum firsthand when my family helped pack holiday baskets for our church's food pantry. Parishioners donate the groceries, and most of us are eager to buy as much as possible for the money. Yet many of the families we serve suffer from the low-income trinity of obesity, hypertension and diabetes. All caused in no small part by diets high in processed food. They don't need the cheapest food we can give them; they need the best. This means that a can of peaches doused in heavy syrup or can of chicken soup embalmed with 980 mg. of sodium per serving isn't doing them any favors. Is it ethical, then, to give the poor larger quantities of bad food on the premise that it's more "economical"? Not if it means early death by ravioli.

＊

❋ *New Work and Old Wisdom*

When I first wrote Lisa Rose's story, I thought it would be published in a matter of months. Then the months turned into years, and the book with her story in it — this book — lay fallow. By the time it came together in 2019, I needed to update her latest chapter.

We met in another brew pub, this one in Grand Rapids. It was a down-jacket February day, but Lisa Rose had the same herbal-infused energy and sundress glow as before. And that's something that's hard to fake. If what Lincoln said holds true, "we're all responsible for how our face looks after 40."

The main headlines from her life were as follows. She has divorced and remarried, although Seth lives nearby to co-parent their children. She dropped the surname Starner and goes simply by Lisa Rose — a fitting binomial handle for a plant lover. In her day job she works as a consumer experience strategist for a Grand Rapids health provider. Translated from org-speak, that means improving how health organizations treat patients and respond to their needs. Given her off-the-charts empathy, Lisa Rose must be ideal for that.

Yet, a part of me says there must be digital marketers in Grand Rapids who could do her job passably well. Meanwhile, who but Lisa Rose could write "Midwest Medicinal Plants: Identify, Harvest, and Use 109 Wild Herbs for Health and Wellness" as she did in 2017 for Timber Press? Lisa Rose still runs Burdock & Rose as a side gig, but wouldn't society be better off if she stayed in her shaman's hut fulltime?

Since the shaman's union doesn't offer much in the way of health insurance or a 401K, that's unlikely. And maybe keeping a foot in two worlds keeps her more grounded in both. Either way, she's not giving up on either. "I am hugely a rebel," Lisa Rose says. "I retain this foundational human right, as all people should, to feed and heal myself from the earth. Just try to take that away from me. Just try."

The Invasion
of the Meat Fishermen

For 20 years running, for reasons of economics, togetherness and, lately, middle-age inertia, my brother's family and mine have spent a week in July at a no-frills cabin on the shore of a little lake in Michigan's Upper Peninsula.

The mornings are especially enjoyable. Nancy and I rise early, sneak out the creaky screen door and set off on a three-mile hike through the Hiawatha National Forest. It leads past two lakes fringed with old-growth pines and hemlock that somehow escaped the saw. We never see anyone on the trail and rarely see anyone on the lakes. At least, we hadn't until the morning when we met a fisherman with a secret to share.

We'd stopped briefly at our turnaround point, the fishing access site on Pete's Lake. Usually, we hear only loons and the gentle clap of waves against the knobby roots of white cedars along the shore. This time, a sturdy and well-made rubber fishing boat eased into the shallows. Its lone occupant

159

was himself sturdy and well-made: a tanned, shirtless, shoe-less fellow with a rock-star mane of sandy hair.

"You do any good out there?" I asked.

In fisherman speak that means (a.) I'm also a fisherman, and know damn well (because I was watching) that you just caught some nice fish in that little cove, and (b.) if you're so inclined, I'd love to hear any useful details such as lure type, water depth, speed of retrieve, as well as the size of any fish caught.

Lucky for me, he was flush with good cheer and magnanim-ity as successful anglers are wont to be.

"Oh yeah, had a *fine* morning!" he answered, with a clas-sic Yooper brogue. "Caught and released a two- and a three-pound smallie (smallmouth bass) on a fly rod. I used these little yellow poppers that I tied myself."

We talked fishing some, him the savvy local, me cast in the role of clueless vacationer. He appeared to be in his early 50s and said he was recently retired — the lucky bastard. Then as he winched his boat onto a trailer, I let it be known that in all my years of coming here, I'd never had much luck fishing. It was then, at the risk of mixing metaphors, that he took the bait and threw me a bone.

"I tell you what," he confided. "You seem like decent folks, so I'll give you a tip, eh? If all you've got is a canoe, then try Flapjack Lake (sorry, not it's real name). It's just a few miles from here on 2266A (sorry, not the real road). There's never *anyone* there. It's good fishing and my wife loves it because we always see beavers and loons and eagles."

He was 75 percent right.

The next morning, because I couldn't stop thinking about Flapjack Lake, I asked Nance to sleep in for once. After a mere five-minute drive down a washboard two-track — how had I missed this place? — I found the lake exactly as he'd described. It was secluded and blissful, its misty shores steepled with lofty white pine and spruce.

For a blessed hour, I had Flapjack and its ethereal silence to myself. My casts along the lily pads yielded three keeper bass that fought gallantly before I returned them to the water. Minutes later a nasty little pike snapped my line and escaped with a new top-water lure. Yet he splashed and dashed with such eager fury that I couldn't begrudge him the loss.

The fish gradually stopped biting and my stomach reminded me that it was breakfast time at the cabin. No matter. It had been a blue-ribbon morning, one that proved I could still catch decent fish in the U.P. after all.

Then, as I backed down the gravel landing to load my canoe, the illusion of a private lake vanished. Five guys rumbled up in SUVs and pickups that bristled with brush guards and gear racks. With nimble energy, they hustled their boats and fishing gear into the water.

"You see a 20-inch northern with my $6 Hula Popper in his mouth, lemme know," I hollered out the window. I tried to sound like a young buck, but it's hard to do in a dusty Dodge minivan.

"Oh, don't worry, we'll get your pike," said a rangy fellow with a red bandana and baggie cargo shorts. He was friendly, but cocky; about as insufferable as I'd been at his age. I was happy for them all the same. It brought to mind a favorite passage from "A Sand County Almanac" by Aldo Leopold: "I am glad I shall never be young without wild country to be young in ..."

By day's end, I would reconsider. It turned out that this merry band was staying at the same resort as we were (so much for the secret of Flapjack). That evening, as our kids roasted marshmallows for s'mores, I saw a sight that made me heartsick. In the yellow glow of a porchlight, they held up for the camera three long stringers that sagged heavy with largemouth bass. It was probably all legal. The fish were large enough and they hadn't exceeded the Michigan daily creel limit of five bass per person. Yet what they did break was a natural law that could decimate the fish population of a small U.P. lake.

The U.P. is not Georgia or Alabama, where the greenhouse fecundity of 100,000-acre warm water impoundments has turned bass fishing into a multi-billion-dollar industry. Here in the cold lakes of the north, fish grow much more slowly. It may take a bass nine years to reach the legal size of 14 inches, compared to three years in the south. Michigan Department of Natural Resources research shows that a lake the size of Flapjack (four or five acres) may hold only 50-60 bass in the keeper category. This means that a crew of skilled, hard-fishing anglers can devastate a small lake's spawning population in short order.

This not only spells trouble for the bass population, but for the lake's overall ecosystem. Mature bass eat bluegills. Without enough big bass as predators, a lake's panfish population can explode. And for most of us, the thrill of catching three- and four-inch bluegills diminishes greatly once we're past the 4th grade.

It didn't appear that my neighbors knew or cared about ecological consequences. For two more days, morning and night, they hauled home stringer after stringer of keeper bass. Their body-count mindset brought to mind the 19th century market fishermen who wiped out Michigan's native grayling. Yet instead of filets salted and packed into hogshead barrels, the bass were iced down and packed into plastic coolers. This, after they'd languished in their own slime for several hours before being cleaned in the fish shack. I recall one bass, a beautiful four-pounder, which lay stiff and yellow in the spittle-warm dregs of a plastic bucket. To what end? Believe me, bass taken from a shallow, weedy lake taste as bad as they sound.

It's not that I'd begrudge anyone a fish fry or a shore lunch of pan-fried filets, an esteemed northern tradition. Now and then we *should* catch and eat a fish if only to remind us of our place in the food chain. But why take so many? Why kill so many bass that a small lake may never, at least in our lifetime, recover?

I suppose it's partly because when fish bite like they did at Flapjack Lake it's easy to believe their numbers are infinite.

Nature's abundance can disguise its vulnerability. When it opens its hand so freely, we're tempted to take far more than we need. Plus, this is Michigan, a land vast in natural riches. It's a state, as described by the eminent historian Bruce Catton, "… that grew up on the belief that abundance is forever." The 19th century passenger pigeons of Grand Traverse that we slaughtered by the millions with nets, guns and explosives. The grayling we seined from the Au Sable by the trainload. The vast stands of white pine, billions of board feet, that built half a nation. It all seemed limitless, right up until the brink of extinction. "Inexhaustible," Catton said, "that fatal Michigan word."

On our last night, I visited another little lake, this one just off Forest Highway 13. The action was mediocre, about what you'd expect from a hard-fished place along a well-traveled road. Still, I was happy enough to bob around in a tiny rented kayak and watch a pair of diving loons give me fishing lessons.

As dusk fell, a 17-inch largemouth slurped down my Hula Popper and shook me from my post-supper torpor. First, he dashed and dove into a reed bed. Then he proceeded to thrash and tail-dance across the water in true spirit-warrior fashion. Delightful. You couldn't script a better end to a U.P. vacation.

After I landed him, I noticed something at the back of his mouth. It was a rusted, size-two bass hook. He'd been gigged deep and had either broken the line or someone had cut the line to free him. Whether because of chance or generosity, this moment was mine to savor. He was a true keeper, alright.

But it was the experience, and not the fish, that I ended up keeping. That's something that will never grow stale in a freezer, fishy and forgotten behind a bag of frozen peas.

Born Again, by Lake and Canoe

A mid-90s day in mid-July. Muggy, no breeze, the merciless sun stalled high in the sky like hell's own runaway nuclear reactor. The lawn (which we don't water to spare the aged pump and well) is as brown and spiky as a horsehair brush. My legs itch with gnat bites from an hour's worth of weeding in the garden.

To wash a smelly dog in the side yard no longer seems like an onerous chore.

The water from a coiled black hose that's lain in the afternoon sun must be, what, 150 degrees? No matter; warmly wet is better than hot and dusty dry. Just ask the fresh-bathed dog, who's plenty frisky after panting like a hydrophobia case all day. So much so that my assistant groomer demanded that she be next.

"C'mon Dad, c'mon-n-n-n," Emily pleaded. "It's my turn. Spray me, spray m-e-e-e-e!"

This is why you have kids, right? Saturday afternoon, a father equipped for watery combat, his target dressed for battle in swim goggles and a dog-sudsy, pink-flowered swimsuit.

Provided, that is, that the garden hose can spray farther than 10 feet. Which ours can't, thanks to the feeble water pressure. Having been farmhouse raised, Emily doesn't know enough to expect better, which made me feel all the worse.

To compensate, I came up with a low-psi alternative. I filled a five-gallon plastic bucket with water and dumped it on her head. The poor kid loved it. Even if it took my pathetic spray rig three minutes to fill the pail. But it was then that a memory of aquatic delight surfaced from my subconscious, like a silver submarine emerging from the depths. I knew exactly what we had to do next.

"Hey, Moe," I said, using her family nickname, "how about we go swamp a canoe? We won't even have to paddle. We'll just fill it with water and swim it around Clear Lake."

The no-paddle guarantee was necessary because it was in said canoe that she had her first brush with mortality. Or so she and her mother would have you believe.

A month earlier, we had tent-camped for the night in our woods on the Portage River. We slept in late, and lingered over our customary breakfast of Blueberry Mancakes, cooked on a campfire in my crusty iron skillet. From there it was only a sedate, 30-minute float downstream to the take-out point at Doug and Robin's house.

Although this time, we should've been quicker about it. Ten minutes after we pushed off our two canoes, a pop-up Michigan thunderstorm rolled upriver. It unleashed its fury with a rage of rain, Zeus-like bayonets of lightning and booms of kettledrum thunder.

There we were, caught on open water in a giant, humming electrode (aka 16-foot aluminum canoe), while terawatt bolts of stray electricity buzzed overhead. It sounded even worse than it looked. Abby and I could hear my wife and Emily screaming from two bends upriver. Their shrieks were punctuated by angry gusts that lashed and snapped at the silver maples and sycamores overhead. Once she heard that, Abby started to scream, too. Mass hysteria (like mass nausea) thrives on the power of suggestion.

In 15 minutes, the storm blew out as fast as it blew in. Our canoes reunited alongside a little island and none of us were physically worse for the adventure. But things turned chilly after that, and I don't mean the weather. We have not tent camped or canoed the river since and may never do so again. It is, in fact, verboten to speak of it.

All that to say that the empty canoe, now upturned against the barn, still bore some heavy emotional cargo. An hour later, at a crowded public access on Clear Lake, I dragged the tainted canoe to the water's edge with my two girls in tow.

"Everybody's *smoking* here," said Abby, with a critical wrinkle of her sun-freckled nose. I was about to correct her exaggeration when I noticed that she was right. Most of the adults were happily puffing away. And, most of their vehicles resembled my commuter car: neglected dents and leprous rust that hasn't seen a car wash or body shop in a decade.

Which made me love Clear Lake all the more. It irks me that Michigan lakes, made by the Lord with such egalitarian generosity, are now priced out of reach for so many. Until my early teens, a bare bones cottage on the lake was still affordable to the masses, for rent or purchase. Granted, these were cramped, thin-walled structures with ancient linoleum floors, rust-stained sinks and threadbare furnishings. That suited us fine, because the lake — not the cottage — was the whole point. You were there to fish, swim, boat or lay in the sun. On the doorstep of summer dreams, why would a healthy person languish in air-conditioned frigidity and watch TV? Here again, we hoi polloi had it right. Long live public access sites, cottages for the people and the tobacco-fumed revelry of blue-collar democracy.

Social commentary notwithstanding, I was determined that this outing be uneventful. Which it was, as we eased the canoe into the sandy shallows by the public beach. There was nothing dangerous here, as several kids with plastic shovels and droopy diapers could attest.

Until, that is, I proceeded to tip the canoe sideways and *intentionally* fill it with water.

At this, Emily stiffened with fright. It's what she feared most about this unfamiliar, unstable craft. That it would roll over, sink and leave her helpless.

Except this time, she saw with her own eyes that it wasn't so. The water-filled canoe floated a few inches below the surface, where it wallowed gently like a friendly manatee. It bobbed and hovered, but it wouldn't sink and couldn't sink. In fact, to sink such a canoe by the usual means would be impossible. As I explained to the girls, there's a built-in safety feature that renders it buoyant. Enclosed in the fore and aft compartments are formed pieces of polystyrene foam. They make the canoe stay afloat, even when filled with water.

After Emily saw that, her whole demeanor changed. In her mind, the once menacing canoe was reduced to an oversized water toy. It had lost its power over her. She swam in and around it with a sense of buoyant mastery.

Even if several swimmers around us couldn't quite see the point of that.

"You need some help flippin' that back over?" ask a bearded man with ropy muscles and cutoff denim shorts. I did need his strong-armed help because what we planned next was even more outlandish. After the canoe was right side up and drained of water, we made one more maneuver. This, to fulfill the vision I'd had in our sultry side yard.

Gently, we flipped the canoe so that it floated topside down on the water. Doing so creates an air bubble inside that keeps the craft afloat. I'd first done this 30 years ago at Camp Rota-Kiwan in Kalamazoo to earn a Boy Scout merit badge in canoeing. It's still a stunt that never fails to marvel kids and adults alike.

"OK, girls," I said. "Swim under with me and we'll come up inside the canoe."

By so doing, I knew they'd have to face another trial: claustrophobia. That's the first reaction when you surface inside an upturned canoe. The water's up to your neck with only a few inches of space above your head. It's as if you're stuck in the hold of a ship that's about to sink. I always picture those doomed, third-class passengers — the borscht and sauerkraut peasantry of Eastern Europe — trapped below in steerage as the Titanic went down.

A moment later, once you've caught your breath, you start to see the rare sensory novelty of it all. You're enclosed in a miniature submarine; your tinny voice echoes against the bass timpani of the water below. The people outside sound close, yet oddly faraway. And it's surprisingly bright under there. A gauzy green glow reflects from the lake bottom, which reveals itself in sharp detail. The undulating weeds, the snail trails on the sand, the shimmer of minnow schools that turn and dart as one. It's a glass-bottom boat without the glass.

Once inside, we couldn't help but duck under and repeat the darkness-to-light sensation again and again. We were reluctant to break the spell and turn the little boat right side up again.

By sunset, much had been washed away. The cleansing even drove from the canoe a small army of spiders (another source of household terror) that fled into the water like Irish snakes before the adjuration of St. Patrick. The spiders had made their home in the canoe's fore and aft compartments. As a 1970s Smoker Craft, one could hardly expect it to be airtight.

Wet sandy swimsuits and all we stopped for ice cream in Three Rivers and, back home, the fluffy dog greeted our car in the driveway. We'd slain the heat with lake water that was our Michigan birthright ... and the feared canoe was only a canoe once more.

BLACKBERRY MORNINGS
TO GOLDENROD AFTERNOONS

A Tree's Rebuke
to a Stingy Heart

After four straight weeks of business trips to New Mexico, California, North Carolina and Ohio, I wanted nothing more than to spend a few fruitful days at home. The vegetable garden had grown shaggy with lamb's quarter and quack grass. The overgrown yard had the desperate air of a foreclosed property.

Then there was the serviceberry tree. The purplish-red, pea-sized berries were ripe, and it was one chore that I couldn't wait to wade into. I'd tie a plastic bucket to my waist and pick from the ground and from a stepladder.

We should pause here to say that if you've never heard of serviceberries that's understandable. They grow on a small, unremarkable tree that usually tops out at 15 feet in height. They're native to Michigan (my favorite trees grow on the Lake Superior shore near Bay Furnace in the Upper Peninsula) but are also widely used for landscaping. There's a good chance you'll find one growing happy and forgotten next to your local school, mall, bank or doctor's office. Most of the time, their incomparable fruit either feeds the birds or falls in purple blotches on the sidewalk.

Such neglect is almost criminal, because in my book, serviceberries rival blueberries, cherries or raspberries. I ate my first one 20 years ago, and as a self-appointed serviceberry evangelist, haven't shut up about them since.

Growing my own, however, has been another matter. I was told that serviceberry trees were nearly immune to insect pests and disease and could thrive and fruit with little care. This turned out to be a line of nursery-catalog fiction that I'll never fall for again. In 10 years, the trees I planted had never born much fruit. Either a little white worm would invade the berries, or, in years with a fair crop, a squadron of cedar waxwings would strip the trees bare before their fruit ripened.

But this year, after a perfect spring with neither too much warmth nor too much frost, our largest tree delivered. By late June a purplish-red haze of abundance enveloped it. There was more fruit than there were leaves. More berries than the tree had set for the past five years put together.

I picked them from the ground, while my daughter and niece shinnied into the crown and picked from there. As we worked — and it's the best kind of work, since you eat as you go — I recalled the day when we brought the little tree home from the nursery. Ah, the naïve hopes I'd had for it. They had long since been dashed and the tree was mainly a nuisance to mow around. Except now, through some quirk of the climate, there was this bounty of generosity.

"Dad," said Emily, from her barefoot perch, "this reminds me of that book "The Giving Tree." For any tree, that's a high compliment indeed. This 1964 classic by Shel Silverstein remains an environmental parable for our age and any age.

To recap an oft-told tale, the book begins with a little boy who loves the Giving Tree for its shade, its fruit and the embrace of its branches. Yet as the boy grows into manhood — and this is a dark plot twist for a children's book — he turns avaricious with greed. He no longer visits the tree out of friendship, but for reasons of personal gain. As a money-hungry young man, he picks all the tree's apples to sell in the city. As a new parent, he hacks off its limbs to make lumber for a family home. As a balding businessman, disillusioned with his life and career, he cuts down the remaining trunk to build a midlife crisis sailboat.

At this point, the boy-man has become a malignant and unbearable schmuck. You half-wish the tree would've keeled over and squished him into apple jelly when it had the chance. And now, with the tree's mortal frame diminished, it seems there's nothing left for it to give. Yet when the "boy" returns for a final time, as a feeble, toothless old man, he learns otherwise:

> *"I wish that I could you give you something … but I have nothing left (said the tree). I am just an old stump. I am sorry."*

"I don't need very much now," the boy said, "just a quiet place to sit and rest. I am very tired."

"Well," said the tree, straightening herself up, "an old stump is good for sitting and resting. Come, Boy, sit down. Sit down and rest."

And the tree was happy.

I'm not sure if our tree was this happy while we picked, but I certainly was. It had given us three quarts of fruit, more than enough for a batch of my wife's homemade jam. Even after 10 years, that was a fair trade on the tree's part. I hadn't watered or fertilized it the way urban landscapers do. But as humans will also do, I took full credit for "my" tree's bounty and was eager to show off a little.

A few minutes later, as I walked toward the house with a full bucket in hand, I saw a new neighbor come walking down Moorepark Road. She looked to be Mennonite given her long, plain skirt and white head covering. Surely, she'd be effusive about such a natural wonder as the serviceberry.

"Good evening," I blurted out, "you want to try some berries?"

I handed her the bucket so she could sample a few.

"Oh, my goodness!" she said, "these are quite good. Are you selling them?"

"No," I bragged, "they come from our tree in the backyard. We've got plenty this year."

"Well, *thank you!*"

With that, she walked off down the road — with my full bucket in hand, and thereby every single berry we'd picked that night!

I was too stunned to say that I'd only meant for her to take a handful. It was as if I'd offered someone a single holiday chocolate and they'd taken the whole box. My unintended generosity had likely cost me a year's worth of PBJ sandwiches and jam-slathered cornbread. Next year's lunches and chili suppers would never be the same. Given the tree's meager track record, it could be another 10 years until the next bountiful harvest.

By the next morning, the shock and disappointment had given way to anger. What made this woman think that she could have the *entire* bucket? When we give a gift, isn't it our prerogative to decide how much we want to give?

Due to the limited production of our trees, most of the serviceberries that we use for jam get picked in urban settings. The next day, during my lunch time walk in Battle Creek, I set out with renewed resolve. The trees I once picked from had been torn out during the construction of a new math and science center. Then I recalled some trees that were planted a few years ago by the Episcopal Church. Might they now be mature enough to produce?

They must've been waiting, because they verily shamed me with their bounty.

Within 35 minutes, I'd filled a one-gallon freezer bag with 4.8 pounds of fruit. It was easily twice the amount that we'd picked and given away, against my will, the night before.

It was truly a loaves-and-fishes moment. It brought to mind, with painful acuity, a quote by St. Augustine (354-430 A.D.) that I'd come across a day earlier: "Any good thing that can be shared is not properly possessed unless it's being shared."

Given that timely, 1,700- year-old advice from the former Bishop of Hippo, there was no way I could begrudge my neighbor a mess of berries. Especially since my tree's Battle Creek cousins had found a way to out-give my stinginess.

In deference to their wisdom, I left for the birds and anyone else (including the neighbor who has — ahem — yet to return the plastic bucket) the fruit on the two other trees. What's there to lose? In its verdict, the universe had plainly spoken. It's easier to fill a hand left open in generosity than a fist clenched tight in greed. There are now 23 jars of serviceberry jam in our pantry to prove the sweet truth of that principle.

The Real Culprit that Kissed
our Ash Goodbye

We are an accomplice to this crime, you and me. To these ash trees, now silver skeletons along a river otherwise alive with the Jurassic squawk of blue herons and the staccato chatter of kingfishers. I know, I know, we didn't *mean* to do it. But when I saw that poppy red comforter in a catalog, I had to have it — overnight, of course. It was simply to-die-for. And now, because of my itchy Master Card trigger finger, millions of woody innocents have done just that.

It's bad, because these trees were my elder kin. They were sentinels of long summer nights on the river, ramrod-straight, 30 feet until the first branch, barked columns that held fast the temple sky. The towering ash stood above, before and behind me. The purple dusk seeped through their celery green leaves, alive with mayflies and the slap of rising bass.

Off the water, I'd felt the sweet crack of an ash baseball bat, whose supple fibers sang the promise of a thousand sand lot dreams. I'd seen, too, how an ash limb, when struck on end, splits along its growth rings to form pliable strips that are woven into Native baskets artful and strong. Vessels to carry all the berries and nuts a season can bear. But now the Potawatomi and Ojibwe join the lament, because their sacred basket trees are nearly no more.

The emerald ash borer (EAB) insect that caused this carnage was first detected in the United States in 2002. They were concealed inside wooden shipping crates from China that arrived as cargo at Detroit's Metro airport. With no natural enemies and an untapped source of their favorite food, the ash borers were free to spread with unbound alacrity. By 2020, EAB had spread to 35 U.S. states and five Canadian provinces. They had killed more than 100 million wild and cultivated ash trees along the way.

In urban areas, the ash's shapely, harp-like form had led to its undoing. Ash make handsome street trees, and millions were planted nationwide after Dutch elm disease wiped out the American elm, another signature street tree. That point wasn't lost on urban foresters, who have since changed their tune about street trees. They now plant a diversity of species (just as nature does in a forest) so that one bug or disease won't smite them all.

As with most environmental problems, the ash tree's plight didn't seem urgent until it became personal. For several years I'd watched the biggest ash in my yard for signs of infestation. I had a heartfelt stake in this one, which I'd moved as a sapling from my mother in-law's woods. Sure enough, there came a June day when I saw the first evidence of decline: the d-shaped entry holes that are the emerald ash borer's trademark. Given what I'd seen on the river, I knew my ash would pass from healthy young tree to standing firewood in short order.

After their forced entry, the insects eat down into the soft and juicy phloem (inner bark). They make a spaghetti-noodle maze of tunnels that girdle the trunk and block the upward flow of sap and nutrients. From there, the crown dies out and leaves behind a broom thicket of leafless branches. Finally, the doomed tree sends forth a last-ditch array of green shoots from the trunk, a Prague-spring display of false vigor that can only end in defeat.

Of course, to lose a single ash that you've nursed from sapling-hood is a disappointment. To see whole ranks of them turn leafless and gray along a beloved river, their diamond-ridged bark fallen away in scabrous tatters, was an unexpected grief. I didn't realize there were so many ashes until I saw them all barren alongside the maples, oaks and sycamores.

Then one Saturday, famished after a morning on the river, I came into the kitchen for some leftover venison goulash. There, I veritably stumbled over the larger source behind the ash's devastation. It was a box on the floor that held a new comforter for my daughter's bedroom. The comforter was spangled with bright red poppies. It was just the thing to gladden a teenage girl's heart, and just the motif you'd expect from a piece of bedding made in Pakistan.

As much as anything, the comforter's far-flung origins were

the crux of the matter. We happen to live in the heart of Amish country, where small armies of Yoders and Hochstetlers make enough quilts annually to carpet a small village. And we buy one from 7,000 miles away? This only makes sense because the corporate calculus of our age counts profits, but unloads environmental costs downstream. Yet we consumers are no better, since we demand that price and convenience trump all else. What I wanted was "The World on Time," just as the slogan on the FedEx truck promised. What online shopper — or emerald ash borer — could ask for more?

Now it's true that humans have long traded their wares and introduced exotic species along the way. In the 1300s, caravans of flea-bitten camels spread bubonic plague along the Silk Road of Asia. In the 1600s, Spanish galleons spread tropical fire ants from the Americas to Africa and Asia when they unloaded the soil they used for ballast in exchange for cargo. But the scale of modern commerce has made the spread of invasive species infinitely more complex. Each year, 480 million pounds of cargo flies into Detroit's Metro airport alone. It's no wonder that jet-fueled consumerism catches nature off guard. Under its own power, the emerald ash borer can fly a half-mile or so. Aboard a jet, it can travel halfway around the world at 600 mph. When we cast our lot with global trade, we agree to accept such Faustian tradeoffs.

Still, the one character I refuse to villainize in this story is the emerald ash borer. How could anyone hate a creature so beautiful? They're as gaudy and flamboyant as a bad prom dress. Glittery green above, sparkly gold below, topped by space-alien eyes of deepest ebony. And striking looks aside, they have evolved to fill a distinct niche in their ecosystem. In their native east Asia, the EAB feed only on ash trees that are dead or dying. Over here, with few rivals, they go for the live stuff. But can we blame them for that? Do we malign a Midwest turkey vulture because its tastes run toward putrid venison? Do we act surprised when a boorish uncle spouts his crank political views at Thanksgiving Dinner? No, because we know that carrion-loving birds and dyspeptic relatives will always remain true to their given natures.

As for the three ashes in my backyard, they did what I expected after the EAB onslaught. They sent up pencil-thick suckers, proof that at least their root systems remained intact. It was a sight encouraging and pathetic. I didn't know whether to coddle them or put them out of their misery. For guidance, I consulted several tree care websites. Some experts were adamant that I snip off the suckers and daub their stubs with herbicide. "We need to kill off every suckering ash!" exclaimed one frantic arborist. "It's the only way we can starve the EAB of its food source!"

That sounded too absolute for my blood. I tend to mistrust any advice that uses martial words such as "kill," "every" and "starve" in the same sentence. I am also a let-it-be landscaper, so I let my three afflicted ash trees sucker back at will, just to see what would happen. That was five years go. Since then, the trees have suckered back and then some. They have grown multiple stemmed trunks, some of which are five inches in diameter and 20 feet tall.

Wherever the EAB went, they have so far left my trees alone. This doesn't mean they won't someday return and feast again on their tender trunks. Yet the longer the EAB muddle along in reduced numbers, the less likely they'll run the table as they once did. There simply aren't enough ash trees to fuel the storm that swept through here in 2010. As such, I see no reason to wage an herbicide-happy campaign of ash extermination on my property. The risk of the EAB's return doesn't supersede the benefits that my trees provide here and now.

In "A Sand County Almanac," Aldo Leopold said, "If the land mechanism as a whole is good, then every part is good ... To keep every cog and wheel is the first precaution of intelligent tinkering." In this case, the cogs and wheels include far more than the ash itself. Entomologist Douglas Tallamy writes in "Bringing Nature Home" that ash leaves provide food for an astounding 150 species of moths and butterflies. The ash's winged seeds are also a vital food source for birds and small animals. Even if my trees re-sprout, die back and sprout again, they'll provide sustenance for fellow creatures that have lived in harmony for eons untold. If I douse them with Roundup, all that age-old symbiosis fades away — at least on my four acres.

Plus, there's this about invasive species. When first unleashed in their adopted home, their rampant growth seems unstoppable and we cower at their invincibility. We ascribe to them all manner of superpower traits. Snakehead, the "fish from hell" that can walk across dry land. Kudzu, the strangling vine that made southerners afraid to leave their windows open at night. Then sooner or later, the laws of epidemiology catch up. When invasive species get too big for their ecological britches, their numbers plummet from disease, starvation and predation.

A case in point being our native woodpeckers, which spend most of their waking hours bopping around trees in search of bugs. Do you think they'd overlook an easy meal of EAB adults and larvae? Of course not. Woodpeckers and sapsuckers will tear into dead ash bark with frenzied abandon. When they're through, it "looks like the tree exploded," says Andrew Liebhold, a USDA Forest Service entomologist.

"The EAB has been massively destructive, because most North American ash trees have little or no defense against it," said Liebhold, in a USDA story about his research. "But we can take heart that native woodpeckers have figured out that the EAB is edible. And this new, widely abundant food source appears to be enhancing their reproduction."

A study conducted near Detroit by Liebhold and Walter Koenig, a Cornell University scientist, found that woodpeckers gobbled up as much as 85 percent of the EAB on infested trees. To add insult to injury (if you're an EAB) woodpeckers also use the trunk cavities of dead ash to build new nests. It's no wonder that woodpecker populations have grown steadily since this new protein bonanza came into their diet.

In the divine order of things, it all fits together nicely. One could almost say that where human ecological sin abounds (saith I, who did covet his Pakistani neighbor's bed clothes) then biological grace abounds even more. Apart from the woodpeckers, there's a native parasitic wasp that feeds on

EAB. We also know that some subspecies, such as the blue ash, have proven EAB-resistant. Plant scientists and the nursery trade will hasten this selection process, just as they've bred blight resistant strains of the American chestnut. I don't say this to justify our wanton destruction of nature, which brings needless suffering to myriad creatures and people alike (most often the poor). Rather, I say it to praise nature's resilience and ability to adapt. Which it will do whether humans are around to see it or not.

Meanwhile, it's anyone's guess as to how or when the ash population will recover. It's not a matter of "The World on Time," but the world on its own time. For now, my daughter's comforter remains on a twin bed that overlooks a bug-scarred, but ruggedly resurgent ash tree. It's a good reminder that "free shipping" is never exactly that.

A Young Girl's Guide to Power Tools

At age 12, our daughter discovered that our front yard could be more than a place to turn cartwheels. It was also an evergreen source of income. I'd gladly paid her to mow it, as it freed me up to tend the garden, pick berries or fish the river. It's time, not money, that's the best currency of a fleeting Michigan summer.

There was just one problem: She couldn't start the mower without me. It was a secondhand push model that took three or four Dad-sized yanks before the engine would smoke and sputter to life.

"Dad," she'd say, with a bright, ponytailed sincerity that would soon break hearts other than my own. "What's up with this thing?"

I suppose it could've been a rusty spark plug, clogged fuel filter or fractured electron transducer shield for all I know. But there's another answer that I didn't want to burden her with just yet. The mower won't start because it's a household machine — a soulless, unreliable, and maddening piece of mechanical enslavement.

Own a house in the country, and you'll feel compelled to own plenty of such machines. Chainsaws, snowblowers, roto-tillers, weed trimmers and leaf blowers are the usual suspects. All ideally useful in their own right, yet all encumbered with hidden costs of maintenance, storage and repair. The more you own, the more you'll play wrench jockey to a garage full of expensive, internal combustion ingrates. And, the more they'll burden your spirit like the chains and strong boxes that brought eternal torment to Scrooge's business partner, Marley.

I'd much rather use hand tools. They're a better fit for anyone with a gadget- and noise-averse personality. More on that shortly. First, let me present a litany of grievances against the big four gizmos that rural Americans assume they can't do without:

The chainsaw: This one tops the list, because it's the symbol of rural independence and flannel-shirted manhood. After 10 years in the country, I still didn't have one, so my wife intervened. For Christmas, she bought me a small, cute harmless model that I believe is called a Woodchuck. However, the one thing this Woodchuck wouldn't do is chuck wood. I simply could not make it start and run for any longer than 30 seconds. There was a finicky balance to the choke and throttle settings that eluded me. Not so for my big brother, who speaks fluent chainsaw. In his expert hands, the Woodchuck would bark obediently to life.

"Well," he'd say, "I don't see anything wrong … with the *chainsaw*."

When I finally took the $250 saw into the shop (even my brother couldn't keep it running for long) I was told there was indeed a problem. To fix it would cost $150 and even then, there'd be no guarantees.

"Yessir, that's the trouble with this model," said the mechanic, with a wistful shake of his head. "They don't start good; they don't run good and they're not really made to be repaired."

You don't say. The saw's 27-page, five-language owner's manual failed to mention that.

Fortunately, if all you need each year is a cord of wood to burn in a fireplace or backyard fire pit, then you don't need to own a chainsaw. Just find someone who does and help them out. There's enough Paul and Pauline Bunyans around who love to cut wood, but don't like to lug, split and stack it. In other words, the unglamorous work that's well-suited for un-mechanical types. Since unpaid grunt labor is hard to come by, you can negotiate a fair amount of wood in trade for your services.

The snowblower: According to the Outdoor Power Equipment Institute, the biggest years for snowblower sales come after a severe winter. Yet at least in southwest Michigan, severe winters rarely come back to back. Especially with the onset of climate change, which in the Midwest will bring warmer winters with more rain than snow in the decades ahead.

For the one or two hard snows a year, I can hire a neighborhood guy with a truck and plow to clear the driveway for $35. For anything less than eight inches, there's a heaven-sent solution: the Yooper Scooper. It's named for Michigan's Upper Peninsula, where winter snowfall totals can reach *29 feet* — explaining why some houses in Houghton-Hancock have doors on the second story.

The Yooper Scooper looks like something my Uncle Mill — he, with a flat-top haircut and green Dickies work uniform — would have designed on his lunch break at the metal fab shop. It's a sheet metal scoop connected to an upright handle, like the one on a push lawn mower. You push the snow where you want it, yank back on the scoop, and the load whooshes out clean and easy. No stooping, no heavy exertion, no clutching your chest while someone calls 9-1-1. All for $60, and one good Yooper Scooper can last a lifetime.

The rototiller: We've not bought one of these because the big, hydraulic rear-tine model that I prefer costs $5,000. Every year I rent one for a half-day ($40) to till my garden. About every other year, the pull cord pops off. This requires a 40-minute round trip to the rental store, where I'll be humiliated by a teenage mechanic in a greasy t-shirt who can fix it in 15 seconds. All that aggravation for one day. Imagine the maintenance headaches a rototiller would require if I owned one for the other 364.

The leaf blower: I've never owned a leaf blower, but God does so we use his. We live on a corner lot, with a half-mile of open field to the southwest — from whence comes the prevailing wind. On an appointed afternoon in late October, a lusty gale will blow in from the Great Plains. It's fueled by pure oxygen and bronze-hued sunshine. It must've been a divine wind like this that cast Pharaoh's horses and chariots into the Red Sea. For us, it sweeps clean the yard and deposits 75 percent of our leaves into the vacant field next door. The rest we can clean up with a broom rake and plastic tarp. And this saves me from one of the most pathetic spectacles of 21st century home ownership: that of a harried, middle-aged man chasing four fugitive leaves around the yard with a screaming meemie of a leaf blower on his back.

Now granted, anyone who plows snow, trims trees or landscapes lawns for a living needs The Big Four power tools and then some. As do farmers, loggers and ranchers. Yet for those of us with manageable yards or minor acreage, at least some measure of people-powered sanity can prevail. We can "afford" to hand-split the cord of firewood we burn each year. Or use a wheelbarrow — instead of a motorized ATV — to move household quantities of mulch, brush, soil and stone. Tools like splitting mauls, rakes, hoes, shovels, pitchforks, sledgehammers and pruning saws can do far more than our atrophied notions of labor think they can.

I believe we should redeem hand tools from the marketing-driven notion that they're obsolete and inferior to "real" tools. Those being the kind with fuel-injected veins and crank case hearts. Hand tools are not only cheaper, but in terms of our physical and spiritual well-being, far superior to their fossil-fueled brethren. They combine good work with good exercise, and in the words of Wendell Berry, "Run on what you ate for breakfast." While mastering hand tools does require some measure of patience and practice, so do yoga, fly-fishing, kayaking, surfing, making bread — and even making love, for that matter. I can't say that I'd prefer a power-tooled substitute for any of the above.

In our sedentary Western world, the physical benefits of working with hand tools can enliven us in ways that drugs for hypertension, anxiety and depression cannot. Millions of American workers spend hours on their rear ends in front of a computer, interrupted only by meetings where they sit on their rear ends and talk. And, a host of recent studies show that people who sit for hours suffer the highest mortality from heart disease and cancer. The Centers for Disease Control and Prevention has called "sitting the new smoking." What we need are more hand tools to encourage healthy labor, rather than more machines to "save" us from it.

Beyond that, there's a spiritual benefit to quiet work done in a natural setting that hand tools help amplify. A hand tool, especially one with a wooden handle, directly transmits to our muscles and sinews the holy heft and grit of creation. You feel the twang of rake tines as they comb through leaves, grass and gravel; the clean rasp of a spade as it cuts through sod and bites into the subsoil; the scuffle of a hoe as it loosens clods and culls weeds from a garden. Even the gentle snick of loppers as they prune an apple tree adds sensory pleasure to the task at hand.

With low-decibel modesty, hand tools keep us grounded in the humane limits of our strength. A hand tool stops working when you do. There's no kill switch necessary, no hearing protection needed to protect us from the latent animus of a machine. When I swing a hand scythe around my beehives, I can still hear the scree of a hawk overhead (around 40 decibels) or the slither of a garter snake in the tall grass. Who could detect such subtleties above the banshee wail of a 110-decibel leaf blower?

In "The Screwtape Letters" by C.S. Lewis, an old devil, Screwtape, gives instruction to a young devil, Wormwood. Screwtape wants his protégé to subvert the Creator's plan for love and harmony. Among his strategies, he suggests that Wormwood incite in humans a lust for constant noise as a means to distract them from things above.

"We will make the whole universe a noise in the end ... we have already made great strides in this direction with regards to the earth," Screwtape says. "The melodies and silences of heaven will be shouted down. But I admit we are not yet loud enough, or anything like it. Research is in progress."

Keep in mind that Lewis wrote this before television, let alone computers and smart phones. I believe it's a fiction of our age to think that we can effectively multitask, especially with matters of the spirit. Either we create room for silence and wisdom — which rarely yells and usually whispers — or we don't. As Screwtape explains, "It is funny how mortals always picture us as putting things into their minds; in reality our best work is done by keeping things out."

Of course, how you pass this knowledge on to your kids without sounding like a mothballed-scented crank is another matter. Young people naturally love new things because they're less invested than adults in what came before. Even so, I'd assumed that my bookish daughter would share my aversion toward steely beings with a crank case heart. I begged her to try my beloved hand clippers — the ones that make a musical snip-snip when I trim grass around a tree. She just asked why we don't own a weed whacker.

Then, when I returned from a business trip, she dropped this bomb: "Dad, guess what? I started the mower without you!"

Like last year's cell phone, my services had been rendered obsolete. Which, I suppose, is the whole point of parenthood. Give kids the tools and let them make of the world what they will. We shouldn't suppose they'll do any worse than we did.

Nonetheless, for every generation I hope there will be room for outdoor work that's quiet and careful. The kind done as much for enjoyment as for the tally of leaves raked or weeds hoed. The kind done with simple, honest tools that are content to make human hands their master.

A River Gone Wild in the City

   We live in two worlds, writes Minnesota poet Tom Hennen. The first includes "airplanes and power plants, all the machinery that surrounds us, the metallic odor that has entered words." In the other, "the woods stand so close you can hear them breathing like wet dogs."

   It's Hennen's second world that engulfs me now and, at least here, the two are well met. From where I stand in the current, an inky cloud of minnows glides through the shallows. It shape-shifts like a Navajo deity whenever my raised hand throws a shadow. On a basswood limb above the water, a sharp-shinned hawk waits with lethal patience to ambush an unwitting wren or sparrow. On a downed elm trunk, the purple, seedy scat of a raccoon reminds me that pokeweed berries are again in season. All this in an amber jewel of an urban stream that winds within earshot of cars, homes and people who scarcely know it exists.

It's formally known as the Portage River, one of three that gives Three Rivers, Michigan, its eponymous name. I'm here to fish it on a hot, kiln dry August evening and of this much I'm certain. I'll catch at least a dozen bass, maybe a pike or two, and most likely won't see another soul. That's been my experience for 40-odd years and for good reason. You can't reach these holy waters without a struggle. As with any mortal entrance to paradise or perdition, there's a guard at the gate to exact tribute.

Only it's not St. Peter or Charon the boatman, but a gauntlet of poison ivy, stinging nettles, raspberry briars and some sprawling species of Eurasian vine that must've grown six feet since last Sunday. I confront it all lightly clad, as if dressed for temple sacrifice: old shorts, Detroit Tigers t-shirt and duct-taped sneakers. This isn't trout country, so you can save those $500 waders for the Fortune 100 streams of Aspen.

From the street, I pick my way into the spiteful thicket armed only with a fishing rod to joust away the foliage. I stumble through thorn and bramble, each step its own trial. Then finally comes the river, a cool rush of ecstasy for scratched shins and the desk-bound cares of the day.

The river here, adjacent to a law office parking lot, winds like a comma through a deep wooded ravine. It's no Midwestern Machu Picchu, but its ruins do tell a story of faded human conquest and natural renewal. One hundred yards upstream lies the aging Boys Dam. Fifty yards downstream stands an old powerhouse, a defunct hydro plant once driven by waters from the millpond behind the dam. It hasn't produced a volt of electricity since 1971. It does seem to generate energy of a kind no ammeter can measure, but more on that shortly.

As for the two-story brick law office, it was once headquarters of the R.M. Kellogg Company. It was founded in 1895 by Russel Marion Kellogg, a Civil War veteran with a University of Michigan law degree. The company was once the world's largest supplier of mail-order strawberry and flower plants. My grandmother worked long hours there from March to early May, when the plants were sorted and packed for shipping. In summer, my father hoed weeds in the sandy, mile-long fields by the river where the berries and chrysanthemums grew.

Around the company offices, with a flourish of patriarchal largesse, R.M. Kellogg built the stunning Kellogg Rock Gardens. Its pastel flower beds stretched along a terraced riverbank, a riotous display of product promotion and arts and crafts landscape architecture. The gardens were a bona fide tourist attraction and appeared on State of Michigan maps until the late 1970s. Even now you can see evidence of their glory. A curved wall and grottoes laid with jagged stone; a limestone footbridge over a dry streambed overgrown with myrtle. It's a pretty ground cover, but it's now considered an invasive species. Although here — nicely done, Old Sport — R.M. Kellogg's myrtle holds the soil firm on a steep riverbank prone to erosion.

But for now, these are archeological footnotes for the reel task at hand. It's fish I'm after, and for that you need to wade the river, as it's too narrow for a boat and too wooded to cast from shore. Upstream I go, pitching a gold spinner tipped with a treble hook. The spinner, no less than the dappled shade and delightful crunch of gravel underfoot, adds to the river aesthetic. When cast just so, on a flat trajectory, it lands with a metallic splash that sounds like coins dropped in a fountain.

Best of all, in the low, clear waters of summer you can see the fish strike.

Which a 15-inch smallmouth does in short order, just below the myrtled bank. First, he's a black shadow that zooms from a submerged tree trunk, a U-boat ripple of dorsal fin for his wake. Then ... whammo! Man meets fish, line and rod shudder and the game is on.

He streaks toward a dark tangle of silver maple roots beneath an undercut bank. Just barely do I steer him away from his favorite hiding spot into the open water.

After a few showy leaps and porpoise rolls, he tires and comes to heel. Once in hand, what a righteous specimen he proves to be. Blackish brown above, with olive vertical bands and divine golden rays aglimmer on his cheeks. Then, with a defiant tail flip (the fishy version of a middle finger) he splashes back into the current unharmed.

For the fish, it's a fight for life. For the human — who knows why, perhaps some limbic pleasure center that evolution forgot — the encounter brings deep and abiding satisfaction. That this drama played out in a shoebox wilderness makes it even more rewarding. A mower drones in the subdivision 50 yards away. Bassy hip-hop thumps from monster speakers in a black Chevy Caprice. At water's edge, a 12-inch pipe juts from the bank, a rusty menace that once dumped God knows what into the river.

Although it doesn't do that now. When you're here, everything's perfect. Nothing can harm you, no evil settle in your soul. You happily become a human metronome. Cast and reel, cast and reel, cast and reel … until every bad thought falls away like scales from the eyes of the blind man who Christ cured and sent to wash in the pool of Siloam.

The river has been this way since I first set foot here as a 12-year-old. While I've fished most of its 14-mile length, this stretch still feels like my personal Ganges. It's where I learned to fish as I do and think as I do.

That history began around the next bend, where the waters widen for a commanding view of the dam. You know it's coming, and you hear the roar. Even so, it always feels as if you've stumbled upon an unnamed torrent in the north country.

The 19th century dam was built on a scale that's invitingly human. The water shimmers down in pellucid sheets over its mossy green face, in a mesmerizing way that compels human touch. I sidestep carefully over the low concrete apron to wade in the root beer roil of the tail waters. I can see why my father came here after hot days on the Kellogg farm to skinny dip with his friends.

An eternal mist — the Portage River atomized — hangs suspended over the lather. In the churn below, I catch and release my dozen bass quota and then some. Nothing monstrous, but able fighters all, and as dusk sets in I am sated. In late summer, you fish not just for immediate pleasure, but to store up satisfaction against the cold bleakness to come. This I have done in a forgotten little river gone wild in the city.

It's a warm night, but the waning light signals early fall, a season that's by nature melancholy. I'm here alone, but since most fishers are secretive misanthropes when it comes to sharing their honey holes, that's no reason to feel wistful. Then, as I stood dripping on the shore, I realized that what troubled me was something more existential. There were no boys (or girls) at the Boys Dam.

I recall the days when we'd while away an afternoon here. We'd swim, fish, scream, throw rocks, carom around on a frayed tree swing. It all had a "Lord of the Flies" feel about it. There were no adults; ours was a micro-kingdom ruled and policed by kids. Not that it was all Norman Rockwell-fun. It was the '70s, after all, so more than a few teens drank, smoked weed and dropped LSD in the trippy woods. Yet the point is, we all knew and loved Boys Dam. As a wild, local place we felt a kinship with it that was ours alone.

In the span of two generations, that childhood knowledge and interest in the wild nearby has fallen off markedly. Adults my age are quick to blame the distractions of smartphones and satellite television for this disconnection from the natural world. (Even as we grow ever more enamored of our garage door-sized TVs and cell phones big enough to require holsters.) Still, Nature Deficit Disorder, as so named by author Richard Louv, is a modern reality.

Public health researchers say the lack of self-directed outdoor play contributes to childhood obesity, diabetes and ADHD. It plays into vitamin D deficiency, especially for minority youth in urban settings where it's unsafe to go outside. Beyond the physical benefits, natural outdoor play teaches social skills, creative problem solving and self-regulation. To climb trees, make mud pies or a fort from sticks all foster cognitive learning and growth.

Provided that children have an outdoor place where that can happen. In Louv's New York Times best seller "Last Child in the Woods," he asks a child why he prefers to play indoors. "Because," answers the boy, "that's where the electrical outlets are."

When one views Boys Dam from that perspective, you begin to see what it could be. For starters, *public property*, with access reopened that's been denied since the land around it was sold. It was unofficial park before (even when R.M. Kellogg owned the gardens), so why not make it an official one now? In my mind's eye, I see a hiking trail, a footbridge over the ravine, a fishing dock and boardwalk with a viewing platform for birding.

While we're at it, let's tear out the dam itself. Let the penned up lower Portage run free as it hasn't since the early 1900s. Let the pike and walleye migrate upstream again from the confluence of the St. Joseph River a mile south. Let the river's main course return and let the heavily silted Hoffman Pond revert to wetland or forest.

The Michigan Department of Natural Resources would

second that, as it's now their policy to remove as many inoperable dams as possible. Of the state's 2,600 dams, 90 percent had reached or exceeded their design life by 2020, according to an American Society of Civil Engineers report. As less expensive energy from natural gas, wind and solar gains ground, hydro has become a minor player. It produces only 1.5 percent of the state's energy supply.

As for Boys Dam, when my nephew Nick was an engineering student at Notre Dame, I "helped" with a research paper on small-scale hydro generation in Three Rivers. (As in, I provided the name of a city engineer and county park director who he could call.) Based on similar-sized operations, Nick learned that a refurbished Boys Dam would require a $1 million fish ladder. To refit the powerhouse with modern equipment would cost another $1 million.

At this point, I had to reel myself back in and stop the scheming. It's this kind of mental wrangling that makes me have to fish so much in the first place. It was also getting dark. Rather than wade downstream to my car, I followed the portage trail south toward the powerhouse and street. I was almost to the road when I stopped in my tracks. No doubt it was the pastiche of pink twilight, but there was something about the powerhouse I hadn't noticed before.

It's really an attractive, dignified building. It harkens from an age when even a prosaic piece of architecture — a power plant — was built to enrich the public square. Wine red bricks, with several rows of corbeling near the top, provide staid ornamentation. Four banks of 12-foot-tall windows flood the interior in natural light. Add a soaring, 20-foot ceiling and you have a structure with the graceful verticality one expects to see in a house of worship. A blanket of bittersweet vines can't conceal its classic lines.

Yet it's inside, where every window has been shattered and the turbine and generator hauled away, that the building evokes something otherworldly. Water still rushes in from the pond through a concrete sluiceway. Except that where the turbine and generator once stood, there's a gaping round hole in the floor some nine feet across. Ten feet below that, as if in a primal basement flooded by a subterranean sea, there's a three-foot diameter whirlpool.

It's a frightening thing to stumble across in the twilight, I'll tell you that. Through that gaping hole, a vortex glows white as it roars away into nothingness. It could be a portal to one of the other poetic worlds that Tom Hennen writes about. It's as if everything wild and mysterious about the river has found its way here.

A bit spooked, I take a last fond look through the broken windows at the river. I can't bear to leave yet so I scramble down the gravel bank to where the powerhouse ledge meets the water. With a fishing rod in hand, there's no way any angler could resist the sight.

On cast one, I land a chunky, 11-inch smallmouth, a fine fish and standard Portage River fare. On cast two, I am shocked out of my everyday complacency.

For I have tied into a predator and he's a big one. A northern pike, *Esox Lucius* in the Latin; a freshwater shark, a lanky, fearless fish with a dragon's snout and a mouth full of cartoonish-cruel teeth. He's well over 30 inches and four inches across the beam when I pull him ashore. As he thrashes in the shallows, I've got to reach into his T-Rex grill and remove the treble hook. It's dicey. For a moment, my bare fingers are one snap away from a trip to the ER.

And there's more fish to come. A miraculous draught of them to be exact.

I'm casting now into the boiling water where the draft tube (fed by the vortex) bubbles up from below. It must be 10 or 12 feet deep, the bottom scoured out by the constant discharge. The fish lie here in cool darkness. They're invigorated by the oxygenated water that feeds them a steady diet of nymphs, minnows, crayfish, frogs, snakes, maybe fuzzy ducklings and whatever else the food-processor whirlpool flushes their way.

To feed and hold all day against the current has made them big and strong. They strike with fearless aggression like wilderness fish that haven't seen a lure. It's dark, but I can see a white flash of abdomen as the bass leap and land with a belly flop smack as only big fish can.

I have clearly roused the temple guards, *Piscis Leviticus* in the pig Latin, who minister at the powerhouse gates. I hook five big fish one after another, in a pool hemmed in by a downed treetop. It's like fighting them in a bathtub, maybe 10 feet across with no room to play them properly. Two of them I can't land at all.

Suddenly, it's too black to see anything. That's fine, as I'm a bit dazed and euphoric from my mystical encounter anyway.

I could build three tabernacles here and live contentedly forever, as St. Peter was wont to do on Mount Tabor.

I crawl out through a hole in the fence, careful to dodge poison ivy leaves as big as my hand. Then I'm back on Hoffman Street, as joyful from a good night on the river at 55 as I was at age 12. What an immense stroke of good fortune that this can still be as it was.

As I slosh back to the car, my adult monkey brain starts to yammer on about ideas for the powerhouse. An interfaith chapel perhaps or a meditation room with simple benches. A glass floor over the hole (which frankly could be the end of anyone who fell in). Some prayer flags or humble statues in the way of a Tuscan roadside shrine to an obscure local saint.

And then I have to stop myself for the second time that evening — enough with the masterminding already. Yes, we need the cottage-garden beauty of R.M. Kellogg and the green physical therapy of Richard Louv. And heaven knows we need more wild, local places, free from hectoring adults, where kids can find another version of themselves in nature. Yet we should also know this: there is already a natural plan afoot for the ravine's restoration. The Lord and his blue heron commissariat have seen to that. To hear of it, I listen to the dark current purl against the bridge pilings, where a river's hidden wildness keeps the world forever new.

The Wild People that
a Good Lake Needs

The books that people keep in their homes can speak volumes about their character. Although it's not the glossy coffee table books, or gilt-edge classics on a conspicuous living room shelf that provide much insight. No, it's the oft-thumbed volumes stacked on a nightstand, or within arm's reach of a reading chair, that reveal the most about who we are. Of these, it's the bespoke few that we lend to family and friends that say the most of all.

So, when John Barnes, who I'd known all of *two hours*, lent me his prize copy of "Cache Lake Country" — inscribed with a signed bookplate from his best friend, no less — I knew it was more than a courtesy. It was a book he'd read, re-read and thought deeply about. In no small way "Cache Lake" was a testament to the life he'd lived and hoped to live. And to loan it was worth the risk, because the power of its truth outweighed the fear of its loss.

"Cache Lake" tells the story of John J. Rowlands, a timber cruiser and mineral prospector who worked in the deep woods of northern Ontario. Written in 1946, it abounds in practical woodcraft and a moccasin-shod reverence for nature. Rowlands never reveals the exact location of Cache Lake. He doesn't need to. We don't need grid coordinates to plumb the universal truths of wilderness. It's enough that he shares the fey sense of predestination that led him there:

> *"After I cleared the thoroughfare and came out on the small lake, I stopped paddling like a fellow will when he sees new water for the first time. The sun had come up and mist hung motionless like a big cobweb just above the surface.*

> *"I had sat there perhaps half an hour, like a man under a spell, just looking it over ... This was the lake of my boyhood dreams!*

> *"Then, for no reason I understood, I paddled ashore, built a fire and made myself a pail of tea. And there was a big tree ... a tall white pine just where it ought to be. I knew then I had found the place where I always wanted to be."*

What makes "Cache Lake" so much more than another year-in-the-woods memoir are the warmly limned friendships between Rowlands, Chief Tibeash, a Cree trapper, and Henry

"Hank" Kane, the book's illustrator. They're at once wilderness solitaires and amiable neighbors, who live a mile or two apart as the loon flies. They're also dedicated tinkerers, and whenever they meet for a meal or camping trip, some feat of shade-tree engineering ensues. Spoons made from mussel shells. Sunglasses and a raincoat made from birch bark. A hammock made from barrel staves. A Pinterest-worthy lantern made from a bean can.

Despite their compulsive creativity, the three *habitants* are rarely in a hurry for anything. As Rowlands explains, time doesn't work that way once "a fellow" gets free from the shackles of clocks and calendars:

> *"Time is a strange standard of measure, for its value changes so much, depending on what you're doing and where you are. In the city, most folks are slaves of minutes and hours. Here in the north woods it's different. It is not the hours or days, but what happens at various seasons of the year that counts ... Often, it (time) stops for a while and sometimes backtracks on its own trail."*

Without losing its quiet lyricism, the book offers useful instructions for homemade sleds, ice boats, compasses and canoe paddles, as well as toys, folk art and back country cuisine. All crafted from backwoods flotsam (think packing crates) and native materials (think spruce gum and hemlock roots).

211

I'll never make any of this stuff, except maybe the recipes for griddlecakes and rice pudding. Yet it's not only what's made here that's important. It's the idea that average men and women once possessed such a rich store of unplugged, practical know-how. As an artifact of human ingenuity turned toward peaceful ends, someone should stow a copy of "Cache Lake" aboard the next NASA deep-space module. It would surely impress any sentient life form that happens upon it. The instructions for making a radio from "scrap-pile" parts — tin foil, wax paper, a broomstick, a broken bottle, etc. — are alone worth their weight in stardust.

John Barnes loaned me "Cache Lake" when I visited him and his wife, Jane Barnes, at their home on Pleasant Lake near Three Rivers. It's a pleasant lake alright, especially on an August evening with a pink sky and a light breeze that hinted at evening rain. The barometer was falling, which meant the bass were biting, but I had other fish to fry.

"Tom, come on in, let's go out back and I'll show you around," said John as he greeted me at the front door. Just like that we were indoors and then out. It didn't look like the Barnes' used their front door much, or even their house much, in the summer.

What I saw out back was a sight once completely normal on Pleasant Lake. At least, in about 1890. Along the Barnes' stretch of shoreline, some 120 feet wide and 20 feet deep, there grew nothing but native vegetation. It was a riot of color and form, a tangle of wildflowers, ferns, sedges and low shrubs. It smelled sweetly of new growth and the healthy ferment of decay. And it was all planted just three years ago, where turf grass once stretched to the lake.

It's no surprise that these native plants took root and thrived. Since at least the last Ice Age, this ecosystem had been their home. They evolved here and belong here, as no forsythia from a big-box nursery ever will. Everything about them fits the locale. In "Cache Lake," Rowlands writes of wildflowers that "had stolen their color from the sharp blue sky." It's not only blue lobelia that do that here, but Joe Pye weed that has somehow absorbed the bubble gum pink hues of dusk.

It didn't take long for wild creatures, who know a good boudoir and lunch counter when they see one, to make this pocket refuge their home. To the Barnes' shore came turtles and snakes, frog and toads, and pollinating birds and insects, such as the fist-sized Luna moth, gaudy as a Vegas showgirl. They've found a rare natural spot to rest and reproduce, to eat and be eaten.

"This is nature's pantry out here. Nature has arranged it so that everything is food for something else," said John Barnes, sounding not unlike John Rowlands. "We wouldn't want to live where it's sterile."

No, but many Midwestern lakes do project that image. There's the ring of close-set houses with sloping lawns, well-watered and well-fertilized, that stretch to the water's edge. A few lakeside trees, but not many. Seawalls, made of concrete or steel sheet pilings, where waves slap against an artificial shore. Docks where pontoon and speedboats bob in the breeze, above a lake bottom shorn of aquatic plants and woody vegetation. It's all pleasant enough, with the comely scent of suntan lotion and grilled burgers in the air.

But if looks can kill, then this look may be killing — or at least, wounding — thousands of Midwestern lakes. Instead of close-shorn turfgrass, a lake's wild creatures need leafy edges and aquatic plants where they can feed, hide and raise their young. Instead of vertical seawalls, turtles and frogs need natural shorelines where they can easily move from land to water and back again. And, instead of lawn fertilizer runoff that clogs lakes with algae the color of a kale smoothie, lakes need clean water to support minnows, mayflies and other tiny organisms that sustain life up and down the food chain.

Unfortunately, nature's side of the story doesn't get much ink and that's why I've come to Pleasant Lake. The U.S. Fish and Wildlife Service has paid me to write a series of articles for a special-edition magazine. The USFWS hopes the publication will inspire others to treat their lakefront property the way that John and Jane Barnes do.

For now, the mosquitoes have awakened by the shore, so we adjourn to the side yard. There, we stop to examine some garden statuary that Hank and the Chief might've dreamed up over a "Cache Lake" raspberry cordial (page 156, right before instructions for a bed sheet canoe sail). The statues are part totem pole, part Hobbit fever dream. A bullfrog carved from a stump sits mouth agape, as if frozen in mid-tongue retract by the evil gaze of Sauron. A fierce, great blue heron hewn from the standing trunk of a black locust, looks as wrathful

as Smaug the dragon. As if it might incinerate the next unsus-
pecting TruGreen truck that rolls by.

In the front yard, John points out another example of
nature-powered engineering. A few years ago, he had some
excavation work done on their septic system. It left a depression near the front step where water pooled after a rain. His
solution, inevitably, involved native plants.

"I thought, 'let's do something with that water," said John, a
large man with the build of an offensive tackle. So, he hand-
dug a swale ("Cache Lake" types eschew back hoes) that's
shaped like an hourglass. It's about 18 inches deep and 25 feet
around. All the water that runs from the rain gutters flows into
the swale via an underground pipe. After a storm, most of it
sinks away within a few hours. It stays damp enough to create
a little native wetland, one that attracts yet more bumblebees
and butterflies.

All good, as far as the Barnes' house goes. There's still plenty
of lawn, so their yard doesn't look rat-trap jungly. They have a
nice dock and pontoon boat. They've simply done what they
can to make a harbor of sustainability in a TruGreen world.
But after visiting five similar projects, there's still a question
that no homeowner or biologist has been able to answer: How
much is enough? How much shoreline must homeowners
restore with native plants to keep their lake healthy or help a
sick lake improve?

It's hard to give a definitive answer. A lake's size, depth,
water quality and a zillion other variables make it tough to

design an experiment that would control for all these factors. So, although no scientist would do this, let me offer a proxy. Maybe we should begin not with plants, but with people. As a predictor of future success, ask how many early adopters can be found and recruited on a given lake. Not cultural rebels exactly, but people who may have owned the lake's first recumbent bike or upside-down tomato planter. We're looking for people who — despite social norms that say a lakefront should resemble a putting green — will dig holes in their sacred American lawn to plant what some startled neighbors may consider "weeds."

To be clear, not any early adopters will do. They can't be sanctimonious finger-waggers, quick to green-shame anyone who doesn't think and act like they do. Rather, they've got to be native plant evangelists of the sunniest kind. They've got to sing the praises of praying mantis and humming birds; of oriole nests and turtle nests; of insanely bright wildflowers that will make a yard stand out from the waterfront like no other. They've got to make people green with yard envy, only for black-eyed Susans instead of pop-up sprinklers.

I didn't ask the Barnes where they fall on the tomato-planter spectrum. However, if a lake association wants to promote native landscaping, they'd do well to seek folks with a "Cache Lake" sensibility like theirs. The Barnes' deep affinity for nature far exceeds the usual human fondness for sunsets and Sequoias. Their *biophilia*, as biologist Edward Wilson terms it, took root in childhood through formative experiences in the natural world. It grew into an adult passion for the outdoors and reached full flower in the crazy notion that their yard should become a mini-Yellowstone.

After I'd gotten the lakefront tour, we sat on the deck and talked until sunset. Inside, Jane's 100-year-old mother played cards with her caretaker. She loves to hear waves lap against the natural shore. Outside, as John and Jane sketched the details of their lives together, I began to picture two human vectors as they arced across the graph of a continent.

Both had launched, unknown to each other, from small-town Midwestern origins. John from Parchment, Michigan, with a mother who took him camping and on hikes for spring ephemerals. These early season wildflowers, fragile and oddly distinct, include Dutchman's breeches, which are exactly that: little white pantaloons that hang upside down from the clothesline of a stem. While John's mother showed him the wild world in his backyard, Parchment couldn't hold him. He camped and worked his way out west to study environmental law at Lewis and Clark College in Oregon.

Jane was raised in Toluca, Illinois, population 1,200. Its most notable terrain features are the "Jumbos," two enormous, grassed over heaps of coal slag left from a shuttered mine. Jane's father was a pianist, birder, "early tree hugger" and classmate of Ronald Reagan's at Eureka College in Illinois. And Toluca couldn't hold her, either. Neither could college studies for piano, nursing (five days there) or earth sciences keep her interest. For a time, the only thing that did was trees. They were not, however, the gnarly burr oaks of her native Prairie State.

Her "adventurous streak" also led her west, to the Umpqua National Forest in Oregon. "They asked me, 'Would you like a job as a lookout?' I said, 'Sure! What's a lookout?'" Well, it was work that the "Cache Lake" boys would die for. On a 40-foot tower, all by her lonesome, she'd scan the horizon for smoke plumes, plot any that she saw on an Osborne fire finder, and then call them in via shortwave radio. It was rinse and repeat like that for two summers, from balmy May to chilly October, until the rangers hauled her out on a snow cat.

The human vectors, two Midwest kids wild for the Northwest, would intersect among a group of like-minded friends who cross-country skied and camped in the snow. I can picture the puffy down vests, the lug sole hiking boots, the '70s vintage John Denver hair and glasses. A Cascade Mountain High. Until finally, connection. They were both home brewers, John with his beer and Jane with her wine. "She needed someone to stomp her Japanese plums and that was me," John said. "My toes were stained purple for a couple of weeks after that."

More indelible still was the mutual attraction that followed. By then, Jane had found her academic groove at the University of Puget Sound where she earned a bachelor's degree in occupational therapy. It would become her life's work, just as John would become her lifelong landscaper, lawyer, spouse.

"We made up our minds that we wouldn't live in big cities," Jane said. They acted on that philosophy when they moved for work to Fairbanks, Alaska. Then, in a reverse azimuth maneuver that any fire spotter would know, they resected their course to the Midwest. To Three Rivers, where they've raised a family and John has practiced law since 1990.

Meanwhile, the seeds of horticultural rebellion germinated. They bought their Pleasant Lake home in 1993, and John helped his Fabius Township write one of the first township wetland protection ordinances in Michigan. He organized several public fora on lakescaping, even if "more people came from outside the county than from our lake."

To pontificate is one thing, to plant what you preach is another. It was time to go all in. The Barnes' bought 38 flats of native plants, 40 species in all, and hired a native landscaper. From the start, curb appeal mattered. "We wanted it to look intentional, not turn people off because we stuck in a few spindly plants," John said. "My hope was that we'd put in something beautiful that other people would want to follow. This wasn't the old hippy environmentalism."

Yet here's the thing about native plants: They're fiscal conservatives. They won't overspend their capital on leaves and flowers until they've banked an ample sum of below ground energy. For the first few seasons, they plunge their solar earnings into roots, deep roots. Six feet deep for big bluestem prairie grass. Sure enough, after the Barnes mulched and weeded for two years, "boom, they came on like gangbusters."

For John, so beholden to billable hours in his law practice, it must be liberating to let time "backtrack on its own trail," as he putters by the lake. The only clients to please here are the seasons. For Jane, now retired from OT, it's a new occupation that provides its own therapy. "I like being on my knees with pruners," she said. "I let things stand dead in winter for the birds. Then in spring, I'll cut out all the dead stalks, and the box elder and mulberry saplings."

The visual appeal of the Barnes buffer strip speaks for itself. No less important is what you don't see: no nuisance water fowl or lakeshore erosion. Both of which have become chronic problems on recreational lakes. They're also interconnected, which is something many humans fail to grasp. Not Canada geese, though. They know exactly why a green sward of turf-grass along the waterfront suits their fancy.

From a goose's perspective, think about why that's so. Easy walk-in access from the lake? Check. Plenty of short grass, the kind they can pluck right down to the very roots? Check! Few trees that might interfere with a running, flapping take-off. Check! And don't think the geese aren't appreciative. Why else would they leave behind so many unwrapped packages? Namely, the 2 pounds of gooey green excrement that an average goose deposits in the course of a day.

The North American population of Canada geese exploded from 1.25 million in 1970 to 5.6 million in 2012. To deter them, frustrated lake dwellers employ all manner of potions and gadgets. They use spray-on goose repellant and electronic bird repellers. They blow air horns and air cannons powered by propane gas. For theatric effect, there's a life-sized plastic coyote, complete with "a posable, faux fur tail." It's guaranteed to scare off "mean, dirty" geese — adjectives that wild creatures could equally use to describe humans.

For the record, the Barnes' yard has no goose poop and

therefore no faux coyotes. The wildlife biologists say that they can thank their buffer strip for that. When geese look at dense, upright vegetation, they see a killing field. Geese are vulnerable when on foot, so they avoid brushy places where four-legged predators can hide. All that public service from a buffer strip that runs on sunshine.

Also — at the risk of blaming turf grass for all the environmental ills of Western civilization — neither do the Barnes' have an erosion problem. It has to do with being well-rooted, and I don't just mean living in the same house for 25 years. Their native plantings have brawny roots that may auger down 12 feet, where the citified roots of turfgrass may only go down three inches. When powerful waves sweep ashore, your garden-variety sod will cave into the lake in muddy strips. I've seen it bob there sadly as ski boats roar past on a Sunday afternoon. Not so with buffer strips. Their roots grow stronger and more interwoven with each passing year. They not only resist waves and wind, but act as a nursery and estuary for entire kingdoms of insects, microbes and invertebrates. A monoculture lawn wasn't designed for any of that.

As with goose droppings and mowed lawns, there's a devious cause and effect at work here. When people grow turfgrass to the water's edge, they expose the shoreline to erosion. Then, to stop erosion, they may opt for a costly solution that's just as unnatural: a seawall. As formidable as these concrete or steel barriers may seem, they come with a built-in design flaw. By stopping erosion in one place, seawalls can cause erosion someplace else. It has to do with the physics of wave action. On a natural lake, waves dissipate force as they roll up the gentle incline of a beach or lap against lily pads, rocks and woody debris. But when waves smack into an inflexible seawall, they bounce off with a rolling action that stirs the bottom. This causes a scouring, muddied current to flow "down lake" where it can erode the beach of a neighbor who doesn't have a seawall. And, leave the lake bottom barren of fish and wildlife habitat.

It's never easy, of course, to change how our tech-dominated culture thinks and acts toward the natural world. We've come to see lakes not as living organisms, but as big bathtubs to remake in our own image. We set legal water levels for lakes and manage them by court decree. We fill wetlands, pave vast expanses around lakes, and wonder why the ground can't soak up the runoff from heavy rains and floods. And everywhere, the siren song of growth cries for *more*. We replace cottages with four-bedroom, four-bathroom houses, all built on the same narrow lots. Without room for larger septic systems, the excess sewage seeps unseen into the lake. But the lake knows all — and those 2-pound piles of goose poop pale in comparison.

It's all daunting enough to make a fellow of either gender pine for an escape to "Cache Lake." A place where loons cry beneath a yellow moon, and moose glug about in the shallows for water lilies. Where the curl of smoke from a distant chimney calls friends to hike or canoe over for some dinner and hand-whittled conversation. We miss this paradise, even if we've never seen it. Hence, a souvenir industry devoted to cabin trinkets and décor, like the polyresin "Welcome" bears on my hearth.

John Rowlands re-created that world when he wrote "Cache Lake." He did so wonderfully, and that's why we want to go there. But — spoiler alert — there's a big caveat. You see, Rowlands never lived on "Cache Lake" with Hank and the Chief. He created the book's fictional structure as a way to frame the story.

In truth, Rowlands met the Chief while on a prospecting trip to northern Ontario in 1911. He stayed with him for parts of five summers, while the old Chief schooled him in the Cree ways of the woods. They became fast friends, and the Chief even offered to adopt Rowlands. Alas, he was bound for the paved world and a career in journalism. Within five years the Chief was dead. Many years later, when Rowlands worked in public relations at the Massachusetts Institute of Technology, he met Hank Kane. The two friends often took camping trips to northern Canada, and *voila* —Rowlands wrote him into the book.

When I first read about Rowlands' literary sleight of hand, it made me uneasy. It felt like I'd been duped. Then as I thought more, I considered how novelists and playwrights often compress true events in their works. All good writing is art, after all. I've since come to believe that Rowlands' motives were born from admirable purposes.

Rowlands was in his mid-50s when he wrote "Cache Lake."

The days when he'd sleep under the stars on a bed of balsam boughs, wrapped only in two Hudson Bay blankets in the 30-below cold, were well behind him. His youth was gone, and the Chief was gone. Yet in the happy hunting ground of "Cache Lake," their friendship could live forever. The Chief, his would-be father, could take a shine to Hank, just as he had to the young Rowlands. Their knowledge, and spirit of the trail, could teach and edify those over-burdened by civilized cares. That's still what makes "Cache Lake" so relevant. It's full of peaceful, possible dreams. It invites reflection, while it guides readers to try feats of woodcraft that will raise more than a few righteous blood blisters.

I see why the Barneses love "Cache Lake." I see why it appeals to me, a guy who ostensibly wrote six stories to change how people treat their lake property across the Midwest. That's a tall order, since there's 37,000 lakes in Michigan, Wisconsin and Minnesota alone.

The book's unspoken purpose, I believe, is to use natural beauty to convert the world, grandiose and improbable though that may be. Still, it's been done around here before and within recent memory. One profound turnaround happened on the Kalamazoo River, not 20 miles from my home. Coincidentally, the Kalamazoo River runs through John Barnes' hometown of Parchment, which was nicknamed the Paper City for good reason.

By the mid-20th century, the paper mills of Kalamazoo employed 25 percent of the city's workforce. And they were as environmentally disastrous as they were profitable. They clogged the Kalamazoo River with so much unregulated paper solids — bilious, belching and vile — that it could scarcely flow. The river ran green, red or white, depending on the paper produced that day. The noxious fumes were enough to make the paint peel on homes near the river.

After World War II, the river finally caught the State of Michigan's attention. There's a longer story here, ably told by Bil Gilbert in his book "Natural Coincidence." What's most useful for us is how incredibly bad things were, and how unlikely it was that they could ever improve.

At a public hearing in 1950, paper company officials asked that the Kalamazoo be classified as an "industrial river" and set aside as a permanent, open sewer. When told that no such designation existed, they suggested that the State *create* one. Seriously. Their disdain couldn't have been clearer if they'd shouted, "Eff you, Kalamazoo!" with both middle fingers blazing. What most incensed one paper company mogul was the nutty notion that the river he preferred dead would be stocked with trout. This "harebrained scheme," he said, would cost the paper mills "one or two thousand dollars per trout."

Have you ever seen a rainbow trout, coin-bright in a clear river, or lifted with sacramental fervor from the water? The poet Gerald Manley Hopkins did: "Glory be to God for dappled things, for skies of couple-color as a brinded cow, for rose moles all in stipple on trout that swim." It's understandable why those who wholly oppose holy change would fear such pied beauty. Trout in a filthy river, where nothing could live in a 30-mile stretch but sow bugs, leaches and trash algae? It was audacious, ludicrous and shoot-for-the moon exhilarating. No wonder so many people rallied around it.

After 35 years of gradual improvement, the impossible has happened. While the Kalamazoo isn't pristine (too many PCBs in the riverbed for that), it is a thriving fishery for smallmouth bass, and yes, rainbow and brown trout. We have the Clean Water Act and new state and local regulations to thank for that. Yet don't forget those bold citizens who told the paper companies that "they'd have a hell of a time selling that (an industrial river) to the public."

So, maybe getting 10-15 people to plant buffer strips on a lake isn't so daunting after all. Especially if you start small. "The natural entryway for most people is butterflies," John Barnes said. "When you say, 'this is a butterfly garden,' people understand that. It's stunning. Plant butterfly flowers and they really do come."

The Barnes' neighbors have started to ask about plants, and they want to "poke seeds in the ground." They want to attract butterflies and hummingbirds for the grandkids. That's how it begins, with a shared experience of beauty that goes deeper than "pretty." One that evokes wonder and delight and sees harmony in something as creepy as a praying mantis. Discover that and you're not far from the sainted realms of Cache Lake.

And yes, it can happen here. Plant a buffer strip and you'll only "lose" 10 feet of grass by the lake. It's often soggy sod that gets scalped by the mower anyway. It wants to be wet so let it. Give back to your lake a little wildness, and it will make you immensely richer in return.

HONEY FLOW
TO APPLE FALL

Weeds, Seeds and the Sticky Art of Biomimicry

In September, certain plants concoct desperate, even devious schemes to ensure the survival of their kind. It's not enough, as it is with most plants, to drop their seeds and trust that they'll sprout nearby in spring. No, for wanderlust types such as burdock and tick trefoil, the nearby will never do.

To ensure wide dispersal, these plants produce hitch-hike-minded seeds that are designed to travel afar. They will burrow, hook, barb and cling to any human or animal host that happens by. On an early fall walk through an old field or second-growth woods, there's no way to escape them. Collectively known as "stick tights," they do just that to socks, shirts, pants and especially fleece jackets (L.L. Bean must be in league with the burdock/trefoil confederacy). Bushy-tailed cats and dogs are equally prone to their clingy ways.

How one handles such low-grade annoyances reveals much about their character. If you're me, you grouse away as you scrape off stick tights with a butter knife or tug at burdock burrs until — ye-ow-za! — one stabs you beneath the fingernail.

But what happens when a person stops grumbling and starts wondering? Might they encounter, in the midst of an onerous chore, a glimpse of divine engineering? Or even find the inspiration for a multi-billion-dollar industry?

That's what happened in 1941 to a Swiss electrical engineer named George de Mestral, who liked to hunt near Lake Geneva with his Irish pointer, Milka. In the only photo I've seen of them together, de Mestral exudes a classic outdoor chic in his fedora, knit tie and tweed jacket. He holds a shotgun in one hand and scratches Milka's chin with the other.

Picture a golden fall afternoon in the Alps, the crystalline air fresh with the resin of fir trees and the dusty tang of sun-warmed granite. Dog and man have just returned from a tromp through fields that were rife with thistle. De Mestral, a methodical sort, sits on the terrace of his family's estate and tamps a bowl of tobacco into his Meerschaum pipe.

Then, as he brushes the lumps from Milka's tail, the gears in his keen mind begin to turn. He plucks out a burdock thistle, but what others would cast away without a thought, he examines with due care. For he beholds in his hand not a weedy nuisance, but a marvel of natural adhesion and sticky grace. Being the learned sort who owns a microscope, de Mestral decides to take a closer look. It's then that he notices something extraordinary. On the burdock thistle's burrs are tiny hooks that make it almost diabolically sticky.

"Why *yes* … they're little hooks, aren't they? Hmmm. It's no wonder they stick like the devil to Milka's fur and my trousers. What a curious, but useful thing."

And that's how George de Mestral got the idea for a fabric fastener that would connect people to their clothes as never before.

It took 10 years of experimentation before de Mestral brought his product to market. In a button-down world that couldn't see beyond snaps and zippers, his idea was at first ridiculed. But eventually, de Mestral perfected and secured a patent for his invention in 1957. He made two strips of nylon, one covered with thousands of tiny hooks and the other with thousands of tiny loops. Press them together and, sacre bleu — they firmly connect as one. He named it Velcro, which combines the French words *velour* (velvet) and *crochet* (hook).

The burdock that inspired de Mestral came to North America in the 1800s as an exotic species imported from Europe and Asia. Most likely, the burrs were mixed in with hay for livestock. (Although I'd like to think that some stowed away on the unkempt tail of one of Milka's Irish ancestors.) As with many Old-World plants, burdock has great medicinal value. Its roots have been used as a diuretic and topical remedy for skin disorders. In pharmaceutical form, it's been used to make drugs that treat cancer, diabetes and AIDS.

As for the stick tight, it comes from an attractive native

plant known as showy tick trefoil. It's a favored food source for northern bobwhite, ruffed grouse, wild turkey and white-tailed deer. Its showy, pink flowers attract hummingbirds and a host of pollinators. And even more than burdock, the tick trefoil exhibits some pathologically clingy behavior.

We know how the pollination gambit work with most flowers. The colored petals serve as window dressing that lure bees, butterflies and other insects to drop in for a wee dram of plant nectar. While there, they rub shoulders with the anther and stamen, which leaves behind the pollen they've gathered elsewhere and showers them with a fresh dusting of the new. Thus sated, the pollinators buzz off on their botanical pub crawl to fertilize the next flowers along the way.

With the tick trefoil, this reciprocal relationship feels more like a shotgun wedding. When a pollinator lands on a trefoil, the flower's petals *close shut* behind it. Once confined, the flower sprays a coat of pollen on the bug's body. Not until that reproductive chore has been consummated do the petals relax and let the detained suitor free.

The product of this union is a small pod of three to six tick trefoil seeds that resemble those on a redbud tree. A coat of hairs on each seed provides the infamous sticking power. As the plant dries in fall, the seeds sag near to the ground. This makes it easier for a furred creature to brush against them, latch on and saunter off to colonize parts unknown.

A few summers ago, our longhaired barn cat, Zoe, was a wretched mass of burrs and stick tights. As an outdoor cat, she received food, water, dry shelter and basic vet care, but not much else. By late August, her snarled coat hung in matted strips like kitty dreadlocks. It was not only ugly, but a health hazard. Had the strips become snagged and pulled away, they would've torn off the skin beneath. Finally, for $60 — three times more than I'd ever paid for a haircut — we had the cat shaved. Pink and bald as a newborn possum, she spent two weeks indoors before she could grow enough peach fuzz to ward off sunburn.

A clever guy like George de Mestral might see that predicament and come up with more than one way to skin a cat, or at least shave one. But he'd no longer be a lone genius if he did. In part because of de Mestral's discovery, there's now a field of science known as biomimicry. It looks for solutions to human problems in the designs of nature. The lessons learned from biomimicry have led to innovation in fields such as architecture, energy, agriculture, medicine and transportation.

"People are looking for more sustainable ways to do things, and organisms know how to do this," said Janine Benyus, president of the Biomimicry Institute, in a Fast Company video. "After 3.8 billion years, life has learned what works and what's appropriate on the planet."

Benyus points to the veins of a leaf, which she calls, "the world's best water distribution network." She compares its graceful branching structure to the 90-degree angles we use in plumbing and ventilation systems. Those severe turns, she says, cause friction that impedes flow. By taking nature's lead, she believes we could redesign these rigid left or right-tilted systems and make them more efficient. (Plumbers and Congress take note).

To my mind, what's equally marvelous is how nature, unbound by trademarks and patent law, feels free to copy and riff on its own designs. It does so on a scale that ranges from the microscopic to a size whose immensity spans the heavens.

Here's a practical example of that. Look at a leaf, and then at the roots of a tree. Look at an aerial photo of a river delta such as the Mississippi or Mekong, and then look at the veins on the back of your hand. See the similarity? Whether they carry sap, blood or water, whether scaled to the size of a hand or a continent, all follow the hydraulic dictates of Murray's Law. It's an equation that models how nature designs systems of fluid transport.

For another sign of nature's imitative genius, look at a nautilus snail shell. It grows in spiral form, following the same "golden ratio" structure found in a head of Romanesco broccoli. Or for that matter, 100,000 light years away in the pinwheel whirls of the Milky Way Galaxy. Isn't it curious that broccoli and a great spiral of gas and dust should be of the same mind?

Closer to home, a favorite recent example of biomimicry comes from Eiji Nakatsu. Like me, he's an avid birder who greatly admires the graceful ways of kingfishers. Unlike me (a math-phobic dolt), Nakatsu is chief engineer for Japan's Sanyo-Shinkansen 700 bullet train.

During the bullet train's testing, it seems that a sonic design flaw emerged. Due to the mountainous terrain between Osaka and Hakata, the train ran through tunnels for about half of its 344-mile route. As it tore through tunnels at speeds up to 220 mph, the train would cause ear-splitting sonic booms. Nakatsu believed they were caused by a sudden change in air resistance. Whatever the source, the booms had to be stopped. They threatened to damage the hearing (and no doubt sanity) of anyone who lived within 400 yards of a tunnel exit.

"The question occurred to me," said Nakatsu, in an interview with AskNature.org. "Is there a living thing that manages sudden changes in air resistance as part of its daily life?"

Yes, and that thing would be the kingfisher, a small agile bird that I see most summer evenings on the rivers of southern Michigan. While the coloration looks different on an Asian kingfisher, they hunt with all the lethal finesse of their North American cousins.

"To catch its prey, a kingfisher dives from the air, which has low resistance, into high-resistance water," Nakatsu said. "It does this without splashing. I wondered if this was possible because of the keen edge and streamlined shape of its beak?"

After a computer simulation and shooting bullets of various shapes through pipes (great scientific fun, that), the solution emerged. They would re-design the train's nose so that it looked less like a bullet and more like the curve of a kingfisher's beak.

Once they did, the sonic booms stopped and the train rode more quietly. It also traveled 10 percent faster and used 15 percent less electricity. In gratitude, they should've painted the train in a kingfisher pattern, complete with tufted head and white neck ring. It would evoke peace and prosperity, just as kingfisher totem poles do for Native peoples in the Pacific Northwest. It would, as a piece of 220 mph-performance art, personify the left-brain, right-brain mind meld that lies at the heart of biomimicry. But even with an enlightened engineer like Nakatsu, I guess bird-inspired fancy only flies so far.

While the train makes for a hopeful story, it does fall short in one vital respect. If you parked a kingfisher-sleek engine on a rail siding, it would take decades, maybe centuries, for all its steel, glass and plastic to crumble into the soil. Compare that with the beak-to-tailfeather recyclability of a dead kingfisher. Within a month, it will be flat as a penny on a railroad track.

Likewise, we can compare burdock with Velcro. Burdock will fade away with last year's leaves and rise again for seasons to come. Velcro's hooks and loops may linger in the toxic strata of a landfill for 5,000 years, unless some mutant, nylon-eating earthworms come along.

It's all in the execution, I suppose. When de Mestral sought to unravel the burdock's secrets, he acted in the best traditions of science. He observed, hypothesized, tested and applied his findings. He made his first Velcro from cotton but switched to nylon because it lasted longer. If he took biomimicry one step further, might he have found a better substitute — hemp, sisal, jute, donkey hair?

A layperson could be equally creative, even if they have a less commercial end in mind. An eye or ear for biomimicry

— from which engineers make trains and poets metaphors — can also awaken us to the spiritual truths of nature. "Anything," said George Washington Carver, "will give up its secrets if you love it enough."

From a white pine, I would learn how to make needles whir in the breeze like a zither in the courts of King David. From a sycamore, how to slough off the bark of age and wear a crown that gleams white and always new. From a box turtle, how a small home — extravagant only in its lovely, batik shell markings — can carry all that matters most in this world. We can't patent any of that, but its wisdom would profit us all the same.

How to Reply When the Wind Speaks Your Name

The September breeze has decorated our back-yard fire pit with a garland of yellow leaves from a nearby walnut tree. That's a walnut for you. Always the first to call it quits and drop the curtain on summer.

With our fishing poles and kayaks stowed in the barn, I've reluctantly done the same thing. All that remains of summer is a plastic pail of dull stones that someone left on the patio. Could these really be the same red and green jewels that we plucked wet and sparkling from the cold rush of Lake Superior surf?

Eventually, they'll end up in the flower bed — just like the others did last year. No matter. I've already got plenty of Up North tchotchkes to clutter my fireplace mantle. Besides, for this year's souvenir, I brought home something better. A keepsake memory that I should recall every day for the 45 weeks until my next vacation.

The setting was Pictured Rocks National Lakeshore, near Munising in Michigan's Upper Peninsula. It was Friday afternoon, the last day of vacation. While I'd enjoyed the week, a part of me had never let go. I'd yet to feel deeply relaxed, that moment of blissful detachment when recreation becomes true re-creation. You know how it is in those agonizing dreams when you're trying to outrun something bad, but can't make your legs move fast enough? On an over-wrought vacation, the opposite holds true. You can't stop running long enough to enjoy the good that you came to find.

But you keep searching anyway. While the family swam and combed the beach for agates, I wandered down a hiking trail near Miner's River. It led through a dark stand of hemlock, but it wasn't wilderness. It was too close to the beach and parking lot for that. The river, too, was pleasant but unremarkable, like dozens of knee-deep, tea-colored streams in the U.P.

Then as I veered off the main trail to visit the river, something stopped me in my tracks. It wasn't really a breeze — more like a fragrant exhalation from the woods itself. The air was deliciously hot, dry and sun-cured, sweet with the turpentine aroma of pine sap. Above the water, a circular wisp had swept two yellow butterflies into a thermal updraft. They rose in a delicate spiral, a DNA helix come to life. It was an aerial ballet, I tell you. The butterflies mirrored each other's moves as if choreographed. It was so human that it almost seemed creepy.

With that, something finally broke loose within me and fell away like scales from a long-closed bud. It brought a quickening to the spirit. The world at hand, the one I'd driven 500 miles to explore and enjoy, at last had my full attention. For the first time that week I noticed how supremely comfortable I was in my summer vestments: baggy shorts, faded cap and good walking sandals. How could a person stand to wear anything else?

Everything that meant vacation was right there. The lakeshore, the woods, the U.P. — all the verdant gifts of summer had converged at this singular time and place. Here, in a one-seat shrine edged by shaggy spires of white spruce. You could still hear the rumble of cars on the washboard road to the beach. But the sudden quiet I'd found here was of a different sort. It was more within than without.

It was the stillness I once tried to find through meditation, but never could. It was like the soft, slow beat of an athlete's heart after it spent itself on a good workout. It was like the righteous rest of a man after he's spent himself with his beloved. I must've sat there for 20 minutes, wondering how so much mercy could arrive on the wings of a thing so small.

Like most of us, I'd gone on vacation to *do* things. To fish and to hike and canoe; to rent a cottage on a lake in the woods; to eat pasties and ride the tourist boats out of Munising Bay. I'd taken a long to-do list Up North, but what I really needed was a *to-be* list. You know it's bad when they have to dispatch two yellow butterflies to tell you that.

That "Messy" Garden? Let it Be

The garden looks terrible, but neither nature nor I would have it any other way. For one thing, I can scarcely bear to eat another cucumber. The pickle-sized dainties of July have vanished, their vines now faded to blotchy gray. Left to their own devices, the last cukes have grown to elephantine proportions. These yellow torpedoes want nothing more than to swell, split and spill their seeds.

The broccoli, too, have turned renegade. Gone are the compact heads, the seed-catalog perfection of early summer. The plants send up lanky stalks whose florets have bloomed into bright flowers shot through with Easter-yellow glory. The nectar-starved honeybees and bumblebees go mad for them. As for the tomatoes ... well, they've done what every tomato plant secretly yearns to do. Topple over, no matter how you've staked them, and spill a profusion of red fruit in various stages of ripeness and decay. I've never met an upright tomato plant that wouldn't rather live a slovenly, horizontal existence.

This year, even our skinflint apple and peach trees joined the party. A flukish, mild spring made them bear so much fruit that their limbs broke under the strain. (And this, on trees that are usually a shriveled marvel of bug-ridden parsimony.) Yet without a walk-in cooler, how could we keep so many apples from spoiling? We couldn't. We let the extras fall to the ground as "waste," although the deer, mice, birds, ants, flies and yellowjackets didn't think so.

Such fickle abandon illustrates a central paradox of gardening. In spring, before a garden can produce a calorie of produce, you spend long hours to make it perfect. With mathematical tyranny, you measure the distance between each row and each plant — with a *yardstick*, for crying out loud. A daily weed patrol ensures that any fugitive lamb's quarter, purslane or crabgrass that stands taller than a golf tee gets the yank.

Then by late summer, you happily let the whole thing go to hell in a bushel basket. Why? Was all this neatness just ego wax to show off one's gardening chops to friends and family? Yes, but impressing visitors is only part of it. In spring, this idyll of fussy neatness serves a biological purpose. If they're to thrive, little plants do need protection from the competition of fast-growing weeds. If they're to weather an August drought, thirsty plants do benefit from the moisture that a tidy blanket of straw or newspapers help conserve. (By next year, the snow-soaked papers will have dissolved to papier-mâché mush and all but vanished. Last year's bad news turned with poetic justice to good humus.)

Come October, I'm ready to trade row-bounding thinking

for the still-life, cornucopia jumble of the harvest. We've already stir-fried, frozen, pied and jammed our way through a home-grown summer. My neighbors and family will hide behind drawn curtains if they see me drive up with another sack of tomatoes. Complete with its own cloud of fruit flies. The garden calls us to let it be, and nature echoes that refrain.

Our big walnut tree drops its green-hulled nuts with a pleasing *thunk* on the metal roof of the old pig shed. Bass notes from the steel drum band of autumn. Our maple tree showers the yard with bright confetti each time a westerly breeze stirs its branches. This weekend, I'll spread them foot-deep on the garden as natural compost. The garden has met its human obligations; it's right that we let it complete the full measure of the year.

I know this hands-off approach would drive many gardeners batty. To "clean up" the fall garden, they'd rather take a rototiller and chop that messiness into submission. They want to prevent the spread of disease (a good idea) and eliminate a plague of volunteer seedlings in the spring (more on that shortly). For me, one pass with a rototiller in spring commits enough violence to the garden's seedbed. Healthy topsoil requires a chain of living connections, of rhizomes, bacteria and microorganisms that we can scarcely fathom. Must we chop and pummel the good earth into brown powder that could pass for cocoa mix?

Beyond that, even hothouse-raised vegetable plants with GMO mongrel genes have a destiny to fulfill. They are encoded with a deep, sacrificial need to reseed and further their own kind. So, if you love a good corporate underdog story, then do this: Let the seedling children of last year's plastic-pot imports slip the shackles of capitalism and, as Wendell Berry says, "practice resurrection" in the sunny lassitude of unbound soil.

I am especially fond of broccoli volunteers. They sprout in the chilled loam of April, harden off and then produce firm green heads faster than store-bought plants. Like immigrants everywhere, they're eager to prove themselves in their new home.

Eventually, I'll weed out most of the volunteers, even if I do leave too many. Yet as gardeners, we can do so based on our judgment and sense of ethics. We are not like the cuckolded farmers who buy GMO soybean seeds from Monsanto. They must sign a contract to promise that they won't save seeds from their crop and replant them next year. Vandana Shiva, an Indian philosopher, describes this practice as, "The Life Lord of the planet, collecting rent for life's renewal from farmers, the original breeders." At least in my 600-square-foot garden, I reign as lord (note the lower case "l") and feel no obligation to contracept my rogue carrots or euthanize my stray tomatoes.

We can also learn about selflessness from the witness of a tree that's past its prime. Last summer's drought, for instance, induced a phenomenon that gave me pause. Despite the parched conditions, several blue spruces in our yard wore an unusually thick mantle of cones. Of all years, this seemed like one when they should've conserved their energy. The spruces were clearly heat-stressed. Their needles were dry, like a Christmas tree left next to a woodstove. That they should expend themselves on a bounty of cones seemed a foolish extravagance.

Later, I learned from a botanist friend that this was an act of supreme altruism. The trees were indeed stressed, he said, almost to the point of death. And that's what made them produce more seed (pinecones). They knew that their species' survival was more important than their own. In an unincorporated garden, nature always lets volunteers have the last say.

One of the Oldest Tails
in the World

From Old Yeller to Marley, most dog stories have the same ending, but we keep reading and telling them anyway. So here goes.

It's a sunny fall afternoon, and I'd rather be anywhere but here, kneeling in a stall at the vet's office, as my hand cradles — for the last time — the head of our black lab, Melody. She, the prototype country dog, has left her beloved four acres never more to return.

Mel-Mel had been in the animal hospital for two days, and at this point couldn't even keep down water. She nonetheless thumped her tail a few times when we came in. And, in a shaky, heroic gesture rose briefly as if to leave.

Then she gave us a confused, plaintive look that said, as clearly as any human voice, "I want to go home."

But with two failed kidneys home was a place impossibly far.

"Is it time?" the vet had asked me 30 seconds earlier.

"It's time."

The day before he'd left an I.V. port in her front leg during surgery, because they suspected it would come to this. Now it had.

The vet gently slid his needle in, and after a last little huff of breath, Mel-Mel's life slid out. For once, the euphemism matched the reality: He really did put her to sleep.

On the ride home, I clutched Mel-Mel's leash and soiled, stinky collar to my chest. Then I cried as hard as I did at age 10, when my dog was killed on Christmas Eve. (We grownups are never as grown up as we think we are.) In the days that followed, I learned anew that when a creature we've cared for dies, it's not just their presence we miss. We also grieve the abrupt end of daily routines that seemed mundane, but in hindsight gave our lives no small degree of purpose and stability.

Rain or shine Mel-Mel would greet me when I pulled in the driveway after work. She'd nuzzle up to my hand as soon as I opened the car door. No one taught her that; it was all her idea. And every night for eight years it was my job to shut her in the barn at bedtime. As befits a good country dog, she refused to sleep anywhere else but in a stall with straw on the floor. "Goodnight, Mel-Mel," I'd say. "Daddy loves ya.'" (Yes, I really said that.) Did I gripe long and loud on those gusty winter nights when I had to "barn" a stubborn dog that didn't have the good sense to sleep inside by a stoked fireplace? Certainly. But mostly, to barn Mel-Mel (a verb we invented for that purpose) brought the day to a satisfactory close.

The night after Mel-Mel died, in a fit of melodrama, I couldn't help but act out the routine a final time. I trudged to the barn, scooped the can half-full with food, and filled the steel bowl that she would never again empty. It was cathartic in the extreme. My primal sobs from this maudlin little ceremony were enough to scare a barn swallow off its roost.

The next day brought a more practical tribute. It was time to harvest honey from our hives and I needed some dry straw to fill the smoker. As always, I got a handful from the floor of Mel-Mel's pen. Only this time I noticed how much the straw smelled like her (or maybe how much she'd smelled like straw.) It struck me that the trampled straw carried not just her scent, but her hair and thereby her very DNA. In the smoker it would burn as incense, and like the symbolism of incense evoked in the Old Testament, carry a prayer offering to the heavens.

Anyone who's read a weepy dog story can guess what that prayer was about. Meanwhile, on Elysian Fields that I hope abound with putrid compost piles and fat, slow rabbits, long may she run. If she can count my coming in dog years, I'll join her there before she knows it.

For Maples and Men,
Big Moves to Ponder

If we think human lives are subject to capricious fate (I didn't choose any of the nine houses I lived in before age 10) then consider the lot of a tree. A seedling or acorn falls randomly to earth. One among thousands may go unnoticed long enough by a deer or squirrel to absorb the vigor of rain and caress of sun. Then with naïve optimism, it thrusts out a green apostrophe of root to take possession of the soil.

All this is no small victory. For where a seed lands and sprouts will dictate its destiny. Forty feet one way could mean rich soil, a life-giving draught of moisture, enough room overhead to grow straight and well formed. Forty feet the other way and it could strike a vein of sterile gravel or languish with a welter of starved seedlings in the shade of a mother tree.

These particulars were on my mind when I set upon a three-foot sugar maple on the Sunday after Halloween. It had clustered with its leggy brethren under an Osage orange hedge across from my brother's house. Its winged seed must've helicoptered in on the westerly wind. In the obdurate way of trees — the ultimate homebodies — it had strayed no further. And in my view, it would never achieve much here. Cramped as it was for space and sunlight, how will it attain the graceful spread and beer-barrel girth one expects from a respectable sugar maple?

By mid-afternoon, I'd moved the sapling to a new fence-row that will help shelter our beehives from the north wind. Here, it has room to grow in spades. A half-acre of open sky stretches overhead and, instead of rubbing branch tips with a half-dozen stunted seedlings, it stands 15 feet from the nearest tree.

"Welcome to the neighborhood, *Woodrow*," I say, indulging my Adamic impulse to name fellow creatures as I see fit. "May your sap rise strong in the spring!" After a ceremonial blessing, I add goat manure, a five-gallon pail of water and straw mulch to tuck him in for the winter.

Later that day I drove into Three Rivers for groceries. It's usually an autopilot task, the kind where your mind's a million miles away. You pull into the store parking lot and can scarcely recall how you got there. This time, a cold breeze pushed a raft of foreboding, bruise-purple clouds across the fall sky. Seasonal change was afoot, and it made me again consider if it wasn't time for a transplant of my own. We've lived in the same rural home for 24 years, a bastion of stability in a hyper-mobile world. But at what point does staying rooted for its own sake lose its purpose? Maybe it's no accident that stability and stagnation begin with the same syllable.

Since my throbbing sciatic nerve wouldn't let me forget the morning's shovel work, I studied the big maples that line the streets. Many are well past the 100-year mark, hollow-trunked yet still hearty of branch and limb. It comforted me to think they were once puny saplings themselves. And I'd once been a sapling here, too. I'd grown from buzz-cut childhood to shaggy teenager on these streets. There was a time when everything and everyone who mattered in my life fell within the boundaries of this eight-block neighborhood. My school was one block from our home on West Bennett. The Rocky and Portage rivers lay two blocks west and east. The downtown was three blocks away, only two minutes by bicycle.

To the left and right were the leafy side streets that tied everything together. Except this time, along with my usual fixation on street trees, I thought of something more warm-blooded. I began to recite a litany of the kids I'd known who'd once lived here. This was a first. To say their names aloud invested them with a sudden and tangible energy. It was as if I'd conjured them up for an afternoon séance right there in my front seat: Affalter, Bacon, Bales, Bence, Boeschen-stein, Boughton, Brewer, Clark, Clay, Coughlin, Cox, DeBoer, Eppinga, Findlay, Jackson, Hoffmaster, Kostas, Krueger, Moorehead, Morris, Mitchell, O'Brien, Phillips, Reed, Rem-ington, Roush, Steiner, Tavernier, Timm, Ward, Webb, West-phal, Yost and Zanter.

To anyone else it was an anonymous list, random as a page torn from an old phonebook. To one who knew them — how they walked, talked, sang, held a bat, even their malodorous body functions — the names rang bright with recognition and detail. I could hear them as once they'd been shouted above the frothy roar of Boys Dam or spat as epithets on the football field in Lafayette Park. They had an air of solemnity, not unlike the names of combat dead chiseled on the marble Civil War soldier statue in Bowman Park. Except these were my childhood brothers in arms, members of a company now mustered into adulthood.

Something about that simple, telling recitation stopped me short.

"My God, but they're all gone," I said to no one in particular. "Nobody's left in Three Rivers but *me*."

Why I'd suppressed this basic demographic fact, I cannot say. I'd known that I was an anomaly: grown, married and with kids, but still living in Three Rivers. In conversations with expat friends, that "still" can hang in the air like an apology or self-recrimination. However, to finally say aloud that you're among the lone survivors was another level of revelation altogether.

To my knowledge, only two on the list are dead. I'm still friends with two others, but they both fled Three Rivers long ago. Most of the rest have vanished from my life or transplanted themselves elsewhere. They did so right out of high school or college, when their roots were still pliable enough to make an easy move.

My big move? It took me to Kalamazoo, a whopping 30 minutes away. I attended university and worked there for 10 years but returned to Three Rivers after getting married. Where I've been ever since. "Didn't fall far from the tree" barely begins to describe it. In all the world's vastness, I'd managed to settle a whole five miles north of my old family home. I didn't even make it outside the town's 49093 ZIP code.

Which begs the question: If you have half a brain, and a tank full of gas, then for God's sake why stay in a small Midwestern town? This isn't medieval France or Saxony, where feudal lords dictate that, I, Thomas the Obscure, must forever trim the tonsures of monks and perform various bloodlettings, as did my barbering father, William of Donut. Hell no. Not in America. Our Oregon Trail is the interstate, and for jobs, schools, relationships, retirement, warmer weather, colder weather, sheer boredom or sheer spite, we'll move and move again.

And move we must to "get ahead." My friend, a corporate recruiter, wrote a book about the right strategy for doing that. From the first job onward, she says, you must look ahead to the next job and the one after that. You must constantly calculate what new project, skill or responsibility will prepare you for the next raise and promotion. Then you plan your work, and thereby your life and next moves, around that goal.

My friend's right, of course. This is career success 101, an accepted credo of mainstream American thought. Millions would have it no other way. Especially at the leadership level, where we have a nation of professional movers and shakers, of high-cultured vagabonds and free-agent ladder climbers. Living in a third-tier place, I've seen this just-passing-through ethos play out in churches, universities and organizations. Sometimes an upwardly mobile leader brings a life-giving infusion of fresh thinking and bold ideas. Sometimes their reforms, dismissive of local conditions and history, inflict undue harm on employees, congregants and communities.

I've worked for a mega-billion-dollar foundation and a golden-domed university where my rooted life has been greatly enriched by the global-mobile class. Suffice to say it's the opportunity, not the weather or culture, that draws them to the Midwest from New York and D.C., from Delhi and Hong Kong. Since there's no "Lonely Planet" guide to explain the corn flake gulags between Detroit and Chicago, it's been my pleasure to help my workplace émigrés fill in the cultural blank spots. To take them bass fishing and sell them my honey. To bring them homegrown tomatoes, recommend reliable carpenters and take them to u-pick apple orchards. And they, to enlarge my heart with their friendship, along with six kinds of curry, epic stories of life in wartime Saigon and tales from their viper-charmed Indian childhoods. They have made me an honorary citizen of places I will never see. They have taught me that a homebody can be parochial without being pharisaical — if we use our local knowledge as a bridge to the wider world. As uber-homebody Thoreau said in "Walden," "I have travelled a good deal in Concord."

So, here we still are. Now what? We came here to find room, and I will say that for a man raised on a 1/8-acre city lot, our four rural acres have felt downright baronial. "I go off now to walk my *lands*," I'll tell Nancy, my jaw outthrust with Thurston Howell unction. Forget that the old house needs repairs of a sort that I've neither the skill nor inclination to master. Roots can take hold in even uncertain soil.

Of course, what parents choose for themselves they also choose for their children. Mine did so when they shuttled us between those nine houses in Michigan and Florida during the first nine years of my life. As things stand, my girls have about two close friends each. None lives nearer than two miles away. If there's a "downtown" for them it's the malls of Portage 20 miles distant. Is it less desirable to have a few good friends than to roam the streets with a pack of them? Out here, there's no alternative. My girls' upbringing has been shaped by the social determinates of open space.

Ask them now, especially my oldest, and she'll say she can't wait to grow up and live in a big city. For Christmas last year, we got her three oversized photographs that spell out the words New York, London and Paris. When I hung them on her wall, they gave me a sad, sudden chill. Will these places swallow her up? How fast could I reach her on the Champs-Élysées if she gets in trouble and needs her Dad?

But I also recall a family trip we took to downtown Chicago. For three days, we'd stayed in a hotel off Michigan Avenue. We'd walked our feet sore through stores, shops and museums, beneath towering cliffs of glass that conspired to conceal the natural horizon. Then Abby said something on the train ride home that gave me pause.

"Downtown Chicago was awful loud, wasn't it, Dad?" she said, as the empty swales of Indiana dune country swept by. "I hadn't thought about how quiet it is where we live."

Country quiet, as her point of reference, has thus been established. It will admit of coyote howl and tractor rumble, but not of police siren and car alarm.

I'm certain that our kids will leave Three Rivers after college and make a good life elsewhere. But wherever they go, some sensory imprint of their rural upbringing will remain. When they lie awake at night and hear a storm roll in, they may recall how silvery drops of Michigan rain the size of carp scales rattled on the steel roof outside their bedroom windows. If there's a sound that leads to a more soothing, delicious sleep, I don't know what it is. I had an Amish crew put the steel roof on for that very reason. Although it's unfashionable to say, I secretly hope they'll someday settle in a home much like this one.

There's an inherent danger, however, for the steadfast who remain behind. When you're too rooted it's easy to become rootbound — and rootbound isn't good. I've seen it with the perennial plants we buy on sale at garden stores in late fall. Pull off the plastic sarcophagus of a pot and you'll find a circular gob of unhealthy roots coiled tight as an angry rattler. Living things are programmed to grow and will half-strangle themselves in pursuit of the freedom to do so.

After 20 years in the same house, I've begun to think it's time for a little repotting myself.

My ideal would be a one-level, renovated cottage circa

1940s, with knotty pine paneling within and fieldstone and cedar shingles without. It would be squat but artful, elegant but unpretentious — an enchanted toadstool of a place, as compact and neatly ordered as the cabin of a ship. A high-efficiency wood stove would give it heat. Square windows that overlook the wooded, reedy shores of a fishing lake would give it light. There'd be a wobbly little dock for a canoe, and on misty summer mornings, a great blue heron would perch there on one bony leg to hunt with his javelin beak for blue gills.

Geographically speaking such a move would only take me about 12 miles southwest of here (provided I can get the old goat who owns the place to sell). Yet psychologically and spiritually, even the next short move will feel like a long haul.

For two decades, our life here has been the antithesis of uprooted. Here are the particulars. Raise two children. Fix up an unfixable farmhouse. Plant 200 trees (45 species total). Learn enough about gardening to enjoy it, enough about lawn care and household mechanics to detest it. See love grow and fear diminish. Watch the black vault of sky over the barn as the stars wheel away the allotted years of one's earthly existence. In what matters most, they have been years worthwhile and true.

To be clear, we actually have two moves ahead of us. One is optional, the other not. Our mortal demise will take care of the "dirt nap" portion. Like falling off a log, really. It's a one-way trip that some 56 million people worldwide take each year. Then, "Into that great void, my soul be hurled," as Bruce

Springsteen croaks in his song, "Nebraska." The Nicene Creed provides enough detail to flesh out the rest of the story, which we can only trust will end in joy and mercy.

As for the second kind of move, it requires that we do all the heavy lifting. And not just the boxes and furniture. Any sort of relocation must balance the virtues of growth with the benefits of stability. To leave such a beloved and well-known place cannot and should not be easy. It's a one-way trip; leave this little shire and there's no going back. But I can also see, with no small trepidation, what can happen if we overstay our welcome.

In town, I see the street maples as a metaphor of conviviality and social cohesion. Out here, on the sandy loam soils of Park Township, the intransigent oaks tell another story. The first thing an oak sapling does is send down a sturdy taproot, a woody protuberance as deep as the tree is tall. If oaks are like ships on a prairie sea, then taproots are their keel and anchor. They bore deep for the moisture to endure July and August droughts that bake the upper soils into parking-lot hardpan. Taproots keep the solitary, open-grown oaks "windfirm" — resistant to gusts that blow in from all directions on a southern Michigan prairie.

Windfirm. That term no less describes my first rural neighbors, who were either retired farmers or farmers' widows. They are human monuments, living stones raised up from their home ground. In their own oakish way, they've endured droughts and hailstorms; weathered spikes in commodity prices that make farmers a prince one year and a pauper the next. Most have never lived anywhere else, apart from their military service. After one neighbor returned from the Army, he vowed to "Never go farther than what I can see from the roof of my barn."

Of this Entish brotherhood, the neighbor I knew best was Harry. He grew up farming with mules and hewed his own archery bows from the Osage orange "hedge" that lines his property. He hunted, fished and trapped his way through the penury of the Depression. He knew the old Potawatomi dancing grounds and found with his keen eye — from a moving tractor, no less — a magnificent collection of 300 arrowheads, spear points and skinning tools. How do you move someone who's as fixed here as the rivers and glacial outwash plains? You can't. The transplant shock would kill him, sure as an amputated taproot could doom even a six-foot oak sapling. When Harry said, "They'll have to drag me out of here feet first," it wasn't a figure of speech. Because that's exactly what they did.

Leaf fall by acorn fall, that's how it happens. One becomes so grounded by inertia that to move seems unthinkable — and finally, emotionally impossible. This, then, is the exit strategy: Get a smaller, newer rural house that requires less fuel to operate — fossil and human. Then, lavish that saved energy on the people and land around us. As old gardeners say, "plant until you're planted."

Of course, to make our farmhouse marketable, we'll have to dig a new well, repair the roof and so on. In general, fix all the annoying shortcomings that we've long endured, but that no sane homebuyer would accept. Which would be much funnier if it were someone else's house.

Yet while such obstacles may detain, they must not ensnare. When the time is ripe, tear off the Band-Aid, dammit. Think outside the sarcophagus. Focus on that post-move lightness of being and the grassless lawn to be.

For such adaptability, the transplanted maples have much to recommend. It's not that they're immune to transplant shock. If a steel-toothed beast (i.e. shovel) gouged you from your home, would you be? Nevertheless, what little maples do well is take hold promptly and get back to the business of living. Their sap can turn into protective antifreeze for the winter. They can antiseptically heal themselves from the wounds of shovels, fire, hail, insects and wind. They can, through mystic feats of vegetative reasoning, dispatch miles and miles of new roots; spider-web fine, wriggling like antennae to find moisture and feed the superstructure that we know as "tree." Such is their unfathomable genius.

In our new fencerow, that sturm und drang begins anew. When spring arrives, a householder with a plastic water pail, outside a home he loves but has never quite figured out, will try to ease a frail sapling's transition. At least, to a point. As a tree, it will need to make its own commitments and compromises with the local world. Come what may, uproot or taproot, who among us isn't called to do the same?

AUTUMN GOLD

TO THANKSGIVING GRAY

November, Good and Gray

We gladly accept the accounting gimmick of daylight savings time when it adds without cost to the length of summer evenings. From June to August, it makes an indoor job almost tolerable to know the sun will linger in the sky to well past 9 p.m., with a slow-motion dusk that can tarry until 10:30.

Then in early fall, by government statute, we pull the rug from under this charade and revert to the Creator's timetable. The gig is up. By next Sunday, dusk will fall at 6 p.m.

To bid the light adieu, I took the dog out for a 45-minute walk tonight, in what tweedy poets once called the gloaming. The woods behind Harry's house were hushed as only they can be in November (at least until deer season starts on the 15th). There was only a scant breeze to waft up the peppery smell of crushed hickory leaves underfoot. Only the purple berries of pokeweed and Virginia creeper remained, the year's last fruits, whose acrid flesh only wild animals can endure.

The abundant light had done its work to warm and feed the earth. It fled southward now, but lingered this evening as if in melancholy farewell to all it had made.

If that sounds overwrought, well, November does that to a person. We know that cold and oppressive darkness are coming. We must suffer and endure much between now and spring. Still, November's wise voice says, "Not just yet. Breathe in, breathe out. Sit on a stump and see." The spent dazzle of October lies scattered beneath the trees like confetti in the streets after Mardi Gras. November's dominant hues are gray; but a good gray, steadfast and serene. November knows there's nothing left for the year to prove — except our gratitude. The entire month calls us to thanksgiving and not just a single, overstuffed feast day.

The dog and I drank this in, but it was dark by the time we got home for supper. And it was a comfort to see the gray still there. It had seeped from the woods to the sky, now pricked with stars. It made the tree limbs look black as they stood in bony-fingered silhouette against the icy canyons of the universe. Perhaps what we perceive as gray comes from ambient light reflected skyward by the Earth. Does it reach the stars eventually? Should we recalculate light years to account for daylight savings time? (I'll hang up and wait for my answer.)

I'd still rather be wading or sweating out my workday toxins in a garden verdant with sun-warmed tomatoes and the sweet snap of green beans. But for now, it's enough to savor the now. By the 11th month, the year and I have both grown timeworn around the edges — and me, with more effort than output to show for it. It's provident that November offers a rest beat before Advent's sometime oppressive cheer, a humble visitation with a reverence all its own. There's no need to dye away the natural reality of it all. I'll gladly take November good and gray, its days as becalmed and wizened as an old monk. It's the honorable color of a season, and of a life, well spent.

Mountain Lyin' — a Predator's Real, and Imagined, Return

For the past decade or so there's been an ongoing argument about whether or not wild cougars exist in southwest Michigan. I have not been convinced either way. From both sides, I will say there's been no shortage of mountain lyin,' if you get my drift.

From the Michigan Department of Natural Resources, we have heard dismissive denials and a "we-know-best" attitude about wildlife. Their message has been that only a DNR biologist has brains enough to identify a cougar when they see one. As for the public, the credibility of their cougar sightings has at times been on a par with sightings of jackalopes and Sasquatch.

One woman posted a photo of a cougar as it ate from an outdoor bowl of cat food. It may have been legitimate. But in the exponentially errant way of the internet, it had lost all local context. The version I saw was said to be taken in nearby Mendon. Bowling alley flat as I know Mendon to be (elevation 843 feet), it was puzzling to see snowy peaks in the background.

Then at a Three Rivers' farm store, I heard a woman insist that a cougar had left claw marks on the back of her neighbor's horse. This second and third-hand degree of separation — i.e. it happened to my cousin's girlfriend's co-worker — is a common hallmark of cougar sightings. And of most urban legends, for that matter.

Yet all the uncertainty may soon be settled by an unlikely judge: the cougars themselves. "It's only a matter of time," says Michigan DNR biologist Steve Chadwick, "before a wild cougar shows up in southwest Michigan."

Chadwick made these remarks during a meeting sponsored by the St. Joseph County Conservation District. It was at the UAW union hall in Three Rivers, the same one where I'd once held my wedding reception. Such events (the DNR forum and to some degree my wedding) attract plenty of sturdy-shoed citizens. But they also draw their share of the curious, the conspiracy minded and the blissfully confused.

Chadwick knows that stand-up talks like this are part high-school science lecture, part political theater. He's learned to answer the most oddball questions with a straight face. That night, he brought along a cougar pelt and a bleached cougar skull that he held aloft with a Macbethian flourish. His talk and slide show combined the basics of cougar biology with the usual DNR lingo about "management practices and carrying capacity."

As I suspected, the real action came during the Q&A session. It began with a few polite inquiries, but they were only a warmup for the main act to follow: a retelling of the unhinged cougar yarns you'd hear over a cup of food-service coffee at the breakfast haunts of Three Rivers.

Audience member: "A fella I know said there's a black cougar over by Marcellus. There's a farmer out there who said he's seen it sneaking around his hog farm."

Chadwick: *"Well, I can't speak to that particular sighting. But I will say that, in the United States, there's never been a single black cougar killed or photographed."*

Audience member: "I know a guy who says he's found deer carcasses hanging from trees by his place. Isn't that a pretty good sign that a cougar did it?"

Chadwick: *"Uh, no, I wouldn't say so. That's something an African leopard might do ... but not a North American cougar."*

Moments later someone felt emboldened to ask if the DNR had brought in cougars to get rid of the coyotes. Michigan is a state where a popular bumper sticker once read: "Support Your Local DNR Officer — With a Rope." So, I understood the conspiratorial logic behind that statement. There's long been an unfounded rumor that the DNR introduced coyotes in the 1990s to thin out the deer herd. The DNR supposedly did so at the behest of big insurance companies, who were spending too much on car-deer collision claims.

What I didn't see coming, though, was a frank response by Chadwick that injected some reality into a conversation gone farcical. It was a reminder of why public officials should now and then face the citizens who pay their salaries. For without this exchange, who would've heard the admission that followed?

"I know for a fact that a friend of mine saw a cougar while he was hunting deer in a blind over by Jones," the man said. He spoke with an even-toned credibility that made people turn in their folding chairs and listen. He even named the hunter — and it was someone who I *knew*. The hunter in question was an excellent brick mason who had done repair work on our home.

"Yeah, I do know about that one and he's telling the truth," Chadwick said. "He did see a cougar. But it was a tame one that the owner had let out of its cage."

That is correct. Some guy west of Three Rivers had a cougar for a pet.

Forget for a moment why anyone would keep, as a companion animal, a killing machine whose two-inch canines can puncture the skull of a horse. Much less "let it out" of its cage as if it were a Welsh corgi that needed a potty break. The larger point was that maybe some of those reported sightings hadn't been bogus. And if a tame, breeding-age cougar was on the loose and found a mate, then maybe ...

Chadwick was quick to point that the DNR has yet to confirm a *wild* cougar sighting in the Lower Peninsula. That would require a clear paw print, DNA sample or trail camera photograph.

But what he said next made a wild cougar in southwest Michigan sound less like an impossibility — and more like an inevitability.

Solitary male cougars, he explained, have migrated more than 700 miles east from the Black Hills of South Dakota. One was killed in 2008 after Chicago police cornered it by an elementary school. In 2010, a cougar was verified in Greene County, Indiana. It was Indiana's first sighting in 150 years.

Biologists say that an increase in western cougars has forced young males to migrate east and seek their own territories. A wild cougar could no doubt find its way to Michigan, although it'd have to run a gauntlet of Chicago-area freeways to do so.

As for the DNR, once tone-deaf to public opinion about cougar claims, they've now changed their tune. No longer do they issue imperious, scientific denials that leave cougar believers fuming. The DNR now investigates all reported sightings and have formed a special cougar team that includes Chadwick. The team attended a week-long training program in New Mexico, taught by western experts who've managed cougars for decades.

When there's a confirmed sighting, such as in the western U.P., the DNR tries to get in front of the story. "When we have the goods, we tell people and we tell the media," Chadwick said. "We're not trying to hide anything."

It sounds likely enough, then, that cougars are coming.

Which leads to the inevitable question: How will people act once the big cats get here?

It's really a matter of the social carrying capacity that Chadwick talked about. Carrying capacity refers to the amount of wildlife that any given habitat can support. A forest, for instance, has the capacity to feed only so many deer before they eat the trees, plants and shrubs to nubbins. As for social carrying capacity, it's more of a psychological measure than an ecological one. It refers to how tolerant people are of wildlife that may pose a threat or nuisance.

For me, to see a majestic predator pad through an oak-hickory forest at dusk would be a peak life experience. For others, the thought of a 150-pound, saber-toothed wraith afoot in the landscape is reason enough to lock the kids indoors and keep a .30-30 rifle handy.

Given these extremes, here's what will likely be the cougar's biggest obstacles.

The first is personal safety — real and imagined. DNR officials say there's an unwarranted fear of cougars, a solitary animal that wants little to do with people. In the past 100 years, there have been "only" 27 fatal cougar attacks in North America. Of these, two-thirds were on Vancouver Island in British Columbia. In the mountain west, millions of people live safely in cougar country every day without incident.

But again, this isn't necessarily about logic or reason. People may not care if they're vastly more likely to be killed by a wild dog, or struck by lightning, then a cougar. Because one anomaly can shoot our sense of statistical security all to hell.

A case in point would be the horror that ended 10-year-old Mark Miedema's life. In 1997, he was hiking with his family at Rocky Mountain National Park in Colorado. As boys will do — and I've been that boy — Mark bounded ahead of everyone on the trail. According to a New York Times account, when his parents and 6-year-old sister caught up to him, "a lion was dragging him into the wilderness." They chased it off, but by then the predator's ruthless work was complete. Mark's mother was a registered nurse, but all her efforts at resuscitation failed.

Social carrying capacity? In some people's mind, one mountain lion in the entire state will always be one too many.

Apart from the fear factor, the biggest opposition will likely come from hunters. They don't worry much about being eaten, but they are concerned about what cougars eat — namely, white-tailed deer. The only predators these hunters want to see are the two-legged kind who pay $31 for a Michigan deer hunting license. They fear that cougars will kill more than their share of local venison.

Except that's flat out not going to happen. In St. Joseph County, hunters bag around 5,300 deer annually. Vehicle accidents claim another 700. By comparison, an average cougar kills about one deer per week. Given the cougar's wandering ways, we're unlikely to see more than one resident per county. Should that one cougar take down 50 deer annually, that would amount to less than 1 percent of the county's yearly harvest.

What's indisputable, however, is that we've been given a second chance. Numerous wild creatures once nearly wiped out by 19th century bloodlust have re-adapted and returned. It's not only cougars (nationwide population of 30,000, up 1,600 percent since the 1950s) that are on the rebound in North America. Also on the comeback trail since the mid-20th century have been black bears (450,000, up 320 percent), gray wolves (5,000, up 610 percent), alligators (five million, up 400 percent), wild turkey (eight million, up 1,500 percent), and the now ubiquitous white-tailed deer (32 million, up 800 percent).

The two words that best account for these changes would be "improved habitat."

Despite suburban sprawl, there are more inviting places for wildlife to live now than during my father's 1930s childhood. In the Northeast, mature forests have reclaimed millions of acres of abandoned farmland. In Michigan and across the country, fewer hunters, and suburban landscapes laden with dumpsters, pet food bowls and barbecue-slathered grills, have set the table for a beastly renaissance.

While this pseudo environment has been created in man's image, that suits Old Velvet Tail just fine. It can also suit us, provided that we temper our lower brain stem fear of predators with a little frontal lobe common sense.

This became clear during a walk down Hutchison Road, in the violet dusk of a November evening. I'd gone little more than a mile when a small light jounced through the black wall of woods beyond the next intersection.

"Any luck tonight?" I said, as I came within interrogation range of the beam. I wear a reflective orange vest while out at night, but never carry a flashlight. The human eye, once adjusted to darkness, allows more range of vision than a cone of artificial light does.

"Saw a few does and a six-point buck, but he wasn't close enough to shoot," the voice said. The hunter cut a striking, if intimidating figure. Like a Caravaggio painting, his camouflaged face shone stark and fierce in the sidelong glare of his headlamp. A .12-gauge pump shotgun nestled with casual lethality in the crook of his right arm.

We talked briefly and I mentioned that late-autumn nights like these, with no wind and little traffic, were ideal for walks in the country.

To my surprise, that agitated him greatly.

"You're just out here for a *walk*?" he said, shocked that any rational adult would take such a risk. "Don't you know there's *cougars* around here? I heard that a guy over by Marcellus (13 miles west) just had one attack his horse."

At the time, I had not heard. But I did know this. I'd just come face-to-face with an armed, camouflaged stranger on a desolate stretch of country road where no one could hear me scream. And I should worry about a hypothetical cougar? I laughed about that all the way home. Then I slept soundly, buoyed by the happy prospect of a tawny killer angel's return.

From the War to the Woods

It was, I suppose, a coincidence. Although in the way of coincidences, there was a whiff of the mystical about it.

It started at 5 a.m. in Albuquerque, where I'd gone for a business trip. I had a plane to catch, but the dry air and some beers the night before had given me a headache. I dug around in the grungy recesses of my shaving kit for some ibuprofen, but no luck.

But I did find something utterly useless to my hungover condition: a little mirror whose blue case was emblazoned with the Big Dipper, bayonet and mountain insignia of the Army's 172nd Infantry Brigade. It was a souvenir from a long-ago visit to Fort Richardson, Alaska. I was in the National Guard then, so the mirror came in handy for shaving in the field. Yet I had long since retired from the Guard, and now stay in urban hotels with bathrooms where three people could shave comfortably.

"Beautiful," I muttered, with throbbing temples. "Why will I

276

drag around sentimental crap like this for 10 years, but forget to buy Advil?"

Why indeed.

The plane landed in Atlanta, where I would catch a connecting flight to Grand Rapids. After an over-priced plate of mediocre pasta, I merged with the throng for a 10-minute slog through the terminal. For most of the way, I was on the heels of the same soldier. Then, at my departure gate, he stopped dead in his tracks and stood transfixed beneath a TV monitor. Across the screen there flickered a CNN story about an Afghan woman who was raped by Afghan police.

You see plenty of soldiers at this airport, close as it is to Fort Benning. They're usually privates fresh from basic training, as gangly and hyper as spring colts. Not this trooper. His boots were run down, his fatigues frayed and grimy; his neck burned angry red by a fierce sun. He wore staff sergeant stripes, which suggested he'd been in the Army eight years or so.

I stole a glance as he watched the CNN story and his face said it all: disgust, resignation, exasperation and a disturbing degree of fatigue for someone who looked to be in his mid-20s. His condition couldn't have been more obvious if he'd taken a felt marker and written "Combat Vet" in black letters across his forehead.

Then as he shook his head wearily and turned away, I saw it. There on his left shoulder was a unit patch — with a bayonet, the Big Dipper and mountains

"No ... freaking ... way," I thought, recalling the mirror. "Of the thousands of people in this airport, the guy in line next to me is with the 172nd Infantry."

It was one of those rare moments when the veil drops away, and fate or the universe or divine will reveals its purpose with unassailable clarity. You just *know*. And since coincidence had so clearly showed its hand, I knew that some deeper connection was inevitable. So, as we waited at the gate, I stole a glance over the soldier's shoulder and looked at his boarding pass.

Of the plane's 150-odd passengers, guess whose seat was right next to mine? It was exactly as goose-bumpy as it sounds.

On the flight from Atlanta to Grand Rapids, I soon learned that the affable soldier next to me was named Adam. And man, was he wound up. He was quick to talk, too quick in fact. He'd long been in the company of soldiers, where guileless honesty and unfailing camaraderie were essential for survival and kinship. Now, outside the warm circle of his tribe, these traits made him appear vulnerable and indiscreet.

But how could it be otherwise? Two days earlier, he'd been in combat. He was, in fact, 48 hours removed from a bare-assed mountain outpost, reachable only by helicopter that sat astride a Taliban infiltration route a few kilometers from Pakistan.

Adam had already traveled 40 hours, nonstop, for a 15-day leave that marked the halfway point of his one-year tour. There was no time to primp: the red dust of south-central Asia still clung to the pant legs of his fatigues. As he spoke of war, his voice — tense and oddly detached — sounded as if he were still there. It was all combat speak, delivered with the matter-of-fact lethality of a front-line infantryman.

"Man, on Thanksgiving Day we were takin' sniper fire. I opened up with a Ma Deuce (.50 caliber machine gun) ... The concussion had me bouncin' off the rocks ... Then we called in some 1-5-5 rounds (155 mm. artillery) and some CBUs (air-dropped cluster bombs) ... A little later, when a chopper flew the BDA (battle damage assessment) they radioed back and said, "Well, you just spent about $1 million to kill one guy.'"

At one time, I'd been a military journalist. It was tempting to listen, and with vicarious bravado, ask leading questions such as my dated military knowledge would allow. But I also know how easy it is for strangers on an airplane to say too much. Especially one who's endured what Adam has. I thought, too, about the reason that fate had plopped me into the seat next to his. Was it to goad a young veteran into reliving gory memories that may haunt his dreams for a lifetime to come?

About then I had an intimation that it was time to divert the conversation. He needed to leave the murderous crags of the Hindu Kush behind and turn his heart toward Michigan. And in November, there's only one thing to ask a rugged guy from the Pere Marquette River country who's handy with firearms.

"So," I ventured, "you gonna hunt deer during your leave?"

That must have been the best question that any person, on any airplane anywhere, could have asked him.

"Are you *kiddin'* me?" he fairly blurted out. "I'll be out tomorrow *morning*! Me and my dad built this great deer blind last year that's like a little *apartment!* Plus, my uncle owns an archery shop, and I've got some great bows, and I love to bow hunt ... and uh, I *really* don't want to touch a gun while I'm home."

No, Adam, I suppose not. Then for the next half-hour we spoke only of wild Michigan: of big bluegills and the lily-pad serenity of wilderness lakes; of the flash of silvery Coho in his beloved P.M. River; of cagey bucks and wily turkeys, things Adam knew, loved, and yes, could hunt and kill with a modicum of honor and grace.

As the conversation began to ease, I noticed something hopeful. With his verbal ammunition from the frontlines spent, the timbre of Adam's voice had lowered a few registers. To speak with such joy of the north woods had been a healthy tonic. While I can't say I knew him, I dare say that he began to sound more like himself — more Michigan boy than locked-and-loaded paratrooper. You could almost hear the whir and rustle of white pines creep back into his vocabulary. Peace. Quiet. The pad of footfalls on holy ground.

There was, of course, still the unresolved matter of the mirror. Although it felt anti- climactic, I felt duty-bound to give it away. Somehow, this inconsequential thing seemed to have led me here. I got up, and in the tiny airplane restroom sink, scrubbed off the years of dirt and soap scum.

"So, Adam," I said after I sat back down. "I've, uh, got this mirror and I'd like you to have it. I picked it up back when the 172nd was still in Fort Richardson."

"Oh. Well, hey, thanks," he said, pleasant, but a bit underwhelmed. "We can't take mirrors in the field (shiny stuff attracts snipers) but this is cool. Yeah, this is cool."

We talked some more about the Army, but mostly of his wife and kids. Then, as if on cue, we both reverted to what strangers usually do when seated side by side on an airplane: ignore each other and mind their own business.

Once we landed in Grand Rapids, I gave Adam a wide berth as we left the terminal. His family was there to greet him. I didn't want to intrude, didn't want to be awkwardly introduced as "Tom, who gave me this uh … this, this *mirror* with my unit patch on it."

I walked alone to the parking garage and that was it. The aperture of the universe, the one that allows us to glimpse briefly the larger meaning of things, had again closed tight. All that remained was a joyful sense that I'd been part of something mysteriously positive, albeit through no merit or intention of my own. The "clean savor of grace," as Thomas Merton termed it. A verse of scripture also came to mind, but I couldn't remember it exactly until I got back home:

> *"For if any are hearers of the word and not doers,*
> *they are like those who look at themselves in a*
> *mirror; … and on going away, immediately forget*
> *what they were like."* (James 1: 23-24) NRSV

In a fierce land like Afghanistan, it must be easy to forget what benign nature looks like. You see a stand of healthy pines, but they're cover for snipers instead of partridge. You endure the privations of snow and cold, but without the civilian ease and cook-stove hospitality of a deer camp. After a while you don't even sound like yourself, because the war has no use for gentle words that describe things innocent and free.

The journey back from such a place may be a lifetime in the making. Some it will break, while others, as Hemingway said, will grow "strong at the broken places." In Adam's case, I hope the healing began, however slightly, when a coincidental stranger held up a mirror to a tired soldier. In that reflection, may he remember anew the green salvation of home.

The Appeal
of a Well-Simmered Life

It's 9 a.m. on the Saturday after Thanksgiving, which seems like a reasonable, civilized time to make apple butter. Yet in my mother-in-law's farmhouse kitchen, 9 a.m. might as well be noon. (Even if we did — ahem — agree on 9 a.m. two days earlier.) When I arrive, a big batch of apple butter bubbles away in her blue enamel roaster oven. A half-dozen quart Mason jars stand warm and sealed on the Formica counter. Doggone you, Marie. She's likely been at it since 6 a.m., her paring knife ablur as she filled bowl after bowl with peels from a bushel of Golden Delicious. I know the routine, because I'm married to the next-gen incarnation of her.

"Oh, apple butter's easy," she says, with an endearing Virginia twang that her Michigan-bred daughters can't hear because they grew up hearing it. "You just peel your apples and cook 'em down on the stove."

Of course, it's not that easy. No more than it's easy to make, from scratch, her angelically light biscuits, for which she has no written recipe. No more than it's easy, at age 78, to push-mow your half-acre lawn on a muggy August afternoon. No more than it's easy to run an 80-acre farm and raise three kids on a school janitor's income, which she did after her husband was killed in a tractor accident. Such acts of creative sacrifice are only easy if you don't count the cost, and are able, through some crucible of spiritual transfiguration, to convert grief, toil and suffering into cheer and generosity.

How she has done that, I have never been bold enough to ask. But in both apple butter and a life well-lived, one can see the same patient reduction at work. The sauce thickens, and the depth of flavor intensifies across the seasons. The spring sun, the bee-swarmed blossoms, the summer droughts and fall frosts — all these mingle with love and mercy, with gain and loss. All that's unessential evaporates away. It's this distilled essence that infuses the final product, whether it's one's character or something you eat straight from the jar with a spoon.

Whatever the end result, it begins here with apples. And for that, it helps if you live next door to an orchard. Marie has done so since 1960, when she and her husband, Howard, moved to Three Rivers, Michigan, from Blacksburg, Virginia. They bought a farm across from Corey Lake Orchards, a 700-acre operation owned by Howard's brother, Dayton, and wife Allene.

"Yes, Zoe and I lo-v-v-e to pick apples," says Marie. Zoe is her dog, a Wookie-like creation of mixed Airedale heritage. "I stand on the mule (an ATV used for farm chores) to get what everybody's missed."

If that's not a recipe for a broken arm or leg — an older woman alone in an orchard, standing in the bed of a small wagon, reaching and straining to pick apples from an unstable tree — then I don't know what is. But good luck trying to stop her.

The picked apples sit in wooden baskets on her back porch, a magnet for bees and yellowjackets on sunny fall days. The Golden Delicious variety she prefers aren't "good keepers," though. By Thanksgiving, even those stored in an unheated mud room can lose their crispness. Yet until January, they'll do just fine for pies, apple crisps, apple sauce and apple butter.

For the butter, Marie first peels the apples and cooks them for 20 minutes in a pot. Then she runs them through a food mill, and hers is nothing electric or fancy: just a saucepan-sized device with a sieved bottom and hand crank. When you turn the crank (which she must've done, what, 1.25 million times?) it turns a paddle that forces the soft fruit through the sieve. Any seeds or skins remain in the pot. At this point, and you can't go wrong either way, you're either left with silky-smooth applesauce or the raw material for the next best thing, apple butter.

Over the decades, Marie and Allene must have made enough cases of apple butter to fill a bread truck. That was before leukemia claimed Allene a few years ago. But she's still here in spirit, her original recipe preserved like a saint's relic in a Ziploc sandwich bag. It's written on lined yellow paper, in Allene's 1950s schoolteacher cursive:

Boil apple sauce until thick enough to heap on a spoon. Continue slow cooking and stirring until liquid does not separate from the butter when put on a cold plate. Fill jars, add canning lids and seal.

Sugar = 1 cup or less per quart of apple sauce
Cinnamon = ½ tsp. per quart
Allspice or nutmeg and red cinnamon candies
(Red Hots) may be added

Alas, all this measured preparation took place before my "late" arrival. Right now, the kitchen is fragrant with apple steam, the old windows foggy with a Currier and Ives artfulness. As the apple butter cooks, it turns a lovely ruddy gold, alive with bubbles and fumaroles that remind me of a mud pot at Yellowstone.

Marie's right: this part is easy. And so is the conversation as she peels another batch of apples. That's something lost in today's headlong rush to use machines for light work that's patently enjoyable. With your hands on auto pilot, the mind's free to converse and reminisce. This holds true whether there are apples to peel, ears of corn to shuck, cherries to pit, beans to shell or firewood to stack. Such amiable chores, done in good company, can become a hearth stone for sharing family lore and memories.

The stories that captivate me most come from Marie's childhood on Spruce Run, deep in an Appalachian holler. She lived there with nine siblings in a home with no electricity or running water. She churned milk from the family cow into butter. She went barefoot all summer and was 12 years old before her father bought the first family car.

"I look back and think, we couldn't have been that poor, but we were. My brothers picked apples, but in an orchard 10 or 15 miles away. They weren't allowed to take even one apple home. Then one day, they brought home a bag of Red Delicious. We thought it was wonderful: We all got one apple!"

One apple. You can understand how someone raised in such grinding poverty could fall prey to nouveau riche pretensions, should they ever come into money. The hayseed largesse of Elvis, with his fleet of pimp-mobiles and guitar-shaped swimming pool at Graceland, comes to mind. Not so Marie. If she overcompensates, it's with the rivers of apple butter, stewed tomatoes and pickled asparagus that flow seasonally from her farmhouse larder.

"It's all a gift," she says. "God blesses us, and we bless someone else."

In this cheery, apple-buttery kitchen, what I didn't expect to hear was a memory that, even 70-some years later, was still raw in the telling. In the 20 years I'd known her, she's always been one to focus on the good. But there it surfaced, as the last batch steamed away in the blue enamel roaster.

It had happened alongside the majestic New River, which flowed just south of the family home. Marie was six years old at the time and babysitting her 13-month-old brother. Yes, she was babysitting. Today, that sounds like a "someone-should-call-Social Services" outrage. In that time and place, it was an economic necessity for big Appalachian families such as hers. Even a 1st grader had her share of family and work obligations to assume.

Not that this made her duties any less fraught with potential disaster.

"It was summer, and I was supposed to be watching the baby," she recalled, wiping her damp forehead with the back of her hand. "But he crawled across the yard and onto the tracks before I even know he was missing."

Minutes later, a Norfolk and Western freight train steamed down the rails, loaded with bituminous coal from the mines that vein the Blue Ridge. She heard the screech and spark of brakes. She heard the screams as neighbors ran from their homes to a tragedy.

"The baby got hit! The baby got hit!"

The train had wrenched to a stop, its wheels at rest ... by *the baby's head*. His skull was fractured. But there was no doctor, no ambulance and no hospital nearby. They called in haste for the local midwife. She was a woman possessed with rare gifts of healing and a deep folk knowledge of medicinal plants. For two days, she ministered and rocked the boy in her arms. Outside, family and neighbors gathered and "prayed without ceasing" (Thessalonians 5-16). And behold, the baby with a cracked skull lived to tell.

Remarkably, it's not so much the miracle of survival that moves Marie now, but her perceived role in the accident.

She still tears up when she recalls how, as a 6-year-old big sister, she shirked her duty. She just can't forgive herself that; after 72 years, the social dictates of mule-powered Appalachia still hold sway. Although being Marie, she also can't help but praise what Providence has wrought from it.

"Bobby still has a steel plate in his forehead above the eyebrow," she said. "And you know, God has used him mightily."

Well, yes. And perhaps big sister no less than little brother. Try her apple butter on warm cornbread to taste the goodness from whence these blessings flow.

Local Man, 54, Kills First Turkey

I didn't know that a 25-pound turkey could be so strong. But this one seemed to have enough flap to carry us both across the barnyard. Even with his wings held fast in a bear hug, I could scarcely contain his fury. His scaly, four-inch claws tore a foot-long gash in my sweatshirt. My advantage was that I knew where we were going: to the steel funnel that hung dripping from a fence post 75 feet away. It was harvest time, and the Thanksgiving reckoning was at hand.

Of course, by modern standards none of this carnage was necessary — let alone desirable.

Come November, vast flocks of stationary, indoor turkeys roost supinely in supermarket freezers across the land. They are conveniently stone-dead. They have been flash-frozen and shrink-wrapped into culinary submission. They've got a red plastic button stuck in their chest that pops-up after the bird's been properly cooked. It's a foolproof, even idiot-proof system for the millions of Americans who cook only one turkey per year. Myself included.

That status quo went unquestioned until the Thanksgiving when we decided to make some gravy for the family dinner. It sounded simple enough. According to my mother-in-law — raised in a Blue Ridge Mountain holler where drinking water came from a spring — you just need some good "pan drippins" and flour to make gravy.

I'm not sure what you'd call the gray, fatty substance that oozed from our store-bought bird. Most likely it was the saline solution, whose ingredients include emulsifiers, vegetable oil, sodium phosphate, starch and "natural flavors." That's what factory farms inject into commercial turkeys to make them juicy. Whatever its hazmat provenance, it surely wasn't pan drippins. At least not in the good-earth, backwoods Virginia sense of the word. Forget the gravy; this crud made the whole entrée suspect.

"I cannot believe," I told my brother, "that we are about to eat the turkey that this vile seepage just came from."

We did eat it, but I vowed that next year would be different. So, I convinced my brother, who already raises chickens for meat and eggs, that he should add a small flock of turkeys to his menagerie.

We bought 13 chicks, and all but one survived until fall. They were a hearty, traditional variety with bronze-black feathers that made them resemble wild turkeys. When the birds began to mature my brother trimmed their wing feathers so they couldn't escape the pen.

Then one September morning, it seemed as if they'd all flown the coop. When my sister-in-law Diane looked out the back door, she saw the whole flock about 25 yards away in the donkey pasture. She told my brother who rushed outside and grabbed his "turkey stick." The stick is an avian training aid of his own making that's every bit as ridiculous as it sounds. He taps it behind his little flock — gobble-gobbling all the while — and herds them into their coop at night. Only this time, his usually obedient charges ran off into the stubble of a corn field.

"Jeffff, Jefffff!" called Diane, no doubt the latest in a long line of wives who have bellowed at errant husbands from the back door of their 1850s farmhouse. "What are you doing out *there*? The turkeys are all back in their pen now."

They had, in fact, never escaped. The other flock, nearly identical in appearance, was made up of wild turkeys. They'd caught the scent of their incarcerated brethren and stopped by to commiserate. Not unlike Sunday visiting hours at the St. Joseph County Jail in Centreville.

A few weeks later, the weather turned cool and it was time for the penned birds to meet their destiny. They'd lived outside since June in a grassy paddock. They'd fattened on milled grain, earthworms, grasshoppers and excess garden cucumbers. They'd felt the cool breeze of morning, taken dust baths on sunny afternoons and roosted at night in a humble, but raccoon-proof coop made of particle board.

We (actually my big brother did all the work) had kept our

end of the bargain. Now it was time for them to keep theirs. We formed a four-person butchering party for the occasion. Besides me, it included my brother, Diane, and my friend Ladislav — he being an artist, naturalist, fishing buddy and unshaven Midwestern incarnation of Tolkien's Tom Bombadil. (And after several shots of Lad's homemade sassafras liqueur, a trip to Middle Earth feels entirely possible.)

Lad and I watched closely as my brother dispatched the first few birds. Then it was my turn to grab one. While the big tom wasn't hard to catch, the short trip from pen to makeshift guillotine proved highly eventful. For both of us.

"Get 'em over here *quick*," Jeff commanded, as big brothers are wont to do. "Don't let him fight so much."

Then he told me, for the 86th time, about the day he came home to find that a red-tailed hawk had preyed on two hens in his chicken yard. Ever the pragmatist, he butchered one of the fresh-killed birds and made soup out of it. It was famously inedible. The flesh was tough, tasteless and rubbery as a tractor tire. "It's all the adrenalin that does it," Jeff said. "Once they get scared, their muscles are pumped full of it."

I hastily folded the turkey's wings, stuck it headfirst into the funnel, then pulled its head and neck out of the bottom. Within three seconds, the butcher knife had done its job with grim efficiency. The carcass flopped in the funnel for 20 seconds or so — a reflexive attempt at escape — and then went forever still.

"I've probably killed 1,000 chickens, but I never get used

to this part," said Jeff, as a crimson stream spattered into the bucket. "I do it quick because I never want to see them suffer."

Ah, the carnivore's dilemma, never more starkly revealed than in a barnyard abattoir. Yes, it's fitting that we feel remorse for any creature that dies by our hand, lest we grow ungrateful for its sacrifice. It's also fitting that many humans forgo animal bloodshed altogether and get their protein from peanuts and chickpeas. It's also instructive to consider how the animal kingdom handles such matters. That neighborhood flock of wild turkeys? There will be no swift blade at the end for them. It's either the slow agony of sickness and starvation, or an ambush by coyotes that aren't morally opposed to eating them one drumstick at a time.

By contrast, my brother had a bond with the turkeys that no one else could have. He'd built their coop, mended their pasture fence, lugged home 50- lb. pound feed bags from the store. He let them out each morning and turkey-sticked them to bed at night. Granted, he was nice to them at first only to become their executioner later, *but ...*

With meatier work at hand, the ethical woolgathering would have to wait. I dipped the now limp turkey into a cauldron of boiling water, plucked its feathers and gutted it. On a chilly afternoon, it felt perfectly natural and pleasurable to warm one's stiff fingers inside a steaming body cavity. I couldn't help but remember "To Build a Fire" by Jack London. In this much-anthologized short story, a Yukon prospector falls through the ice of a wilderness creek. It's 75 degrees below zero and his very life depends on whether he can build a fire. Then, after a clump of snow from a spruce branch snuffs out his last match, he conceives a final, desperate plan. He aims to kill his wolf-husky dog, cut it open, use its body cavity as a hand-warmer and thus save his mortally frozen fingers. It's telling that the dog sensed something dangerous in the man's voice and had the good sense to run away.

Such are the rarified musings that a turkey slaughter turned literary salon make possible.

Afterwards, Diane took in some fresh turkey giblets and sautéed them with onions and minced garlic. The knowledge that they'd functioned as pulsing organs of a lately plucked and headless turkey didn't lessen their flavor a bit. It also helped that she fried them up with a mess of gaudy-orange mushrooms that Lad had picked from an oak stump along Moorepark Road.

And come Thanksgiving Day? Our cooked turkey was less tender than I prefer, but tastier than I expected. You might say it was "turkier" — its flavor distinct, yet somehow familiar; just as honey from our backyard beehives has its own taste of home. And for similar reasons. The turkey had incarnated the same Michigan flyover country terroir: the silvery morning dews and sunflower-gold afternoons; the black raspberries, purple poke berries, and yes, the same dusting of GMO-tainted corn pollen.

Apart from the meat, I am told (not being a gravy man myself) that the gravy was five-star. Instead of a factory-farm oil slick, the pan drippins rendered a golden river that ran down mashed-potato mountains into a cranberry sea. Taken together, it was everything I could want from a turkey-sticked family operation 100 yards down the road. The best food chains — like the best brothers — should be close-linked, as nature intends them to be.

Acknowledgments

After I wrote "Looking for Hickories," many people asked when I'd write another book. That was encouraging, but also a little daunting. It took 45 years to write my first, so why the rush? That "next-book" question would go unanswered for 12 years, about as long as it takes to age a bottle of good Scotch.

That analogy fits, since an essay writer does run a distillery of sorts. An essayist takes the active ingredients of life and boils them down into stories that – hopefully – have an essence of shared truth about them. Yet writing an essay collection isn't like writing a novel, where the plot and characters spring from a singular source of inspiration. With essays, you live your life, take notes and turn them into stories only after you've gathered enough plausible evidence.

When you write part time after work, that's not exactly a speedy process. Several of these essays had to age in the oak casks of my mind for months and years until they were ready for public consumption. If some taste better than others, well, even the best bars will offer cheap house brands alongside the Glenlivet and Johnny Walker Black.

Along the way, I've been blessed by people who helped me with my writing, whether they knew it or not. I am deeply grateful to Howard Meyerson from Michigan Blue, Kerry Temple from Notre Dame Magazine and Jeff Bilbro from Front Porch Republic. They published my work and made it better with their edits and enthusiastic support.

While at Notre Dame, even as a non-scientist, I grew immensely in my knowledge of science through my work with Jennifer Tank, Lindsay Chadderton, Brett Peters, Diogo Bolster, Ashish Sharma, Patrick Regan, Dominic Chaloner and Fr. Terrence Ehrman, C.S.C. I didn't expect to learn about human and animal ethics, but Bharat Ranganathan made sure that I did. I didn't think I could learn about science storytelling in social media, but Alex Hardy helped me see the light.

To others, gone but ever present, I would thank my father, Bill Springer; my spiritual mentors Thomas Merton and St. Francis of Assisi, and my writing exemplars Aldo Leopold, Donald Culross Peattie, Wallace Stegner and E.B. White. Meanwhile, my very much alive mother, Dolores Springer, can claim credit for being the first person on earth to believe that her C- high school student son could become a writer. Thanks, Dolo.

Back home, my long friendships with Peter Ter Louw and Ladislav Hanka have given me invaluable insight into land protection, environmental politics, academic politics (the worse kind) beekeeping, art, fishing and the quandaries of middle-age, Midwestern style. Please Lord, more beers and smallmouth bass with these guys.

For 25 years, I have lived in the same house with my wife, Nancy, and our two daughters. All the while, my brother and his family have lived a mere 75 yards away. In all those years, we have never quarreled and that is one of my life's crowning achievements. (Not that you can ever win an argument with a big brother.) When I hear his rooster in the morning, and smell his woodburning stove at night, I know that all is right with the world.

As for Nancy, she'd rather that I not say much about her in print, so I won't. Except that she's the beginning and end of everything that we have made here. Deo Gratias.

Three Rivers, Michigan
The Feast of St. Joseph
March 19, 2020

TOM SPRINGER lives in Three Rivers, Michigan, with his wife, Nancy, and their two daughters. He has worked in communications at the W.K. Kellogg Foundation and for the Environmental Change Initiative at the University of Notre Dame. He is author of "Looking for Hickories," (University of Michigan Press) and "How to Unravel Science Mysteries for Young Minds Without Unraveling," (W.K. Kellogg Foundation). Most astonishingly, Tom was once a modern dance critic for the Kalamazoo Gazette. In the annals of American journalism, he may be the only former HVAC mechanic and Army National Guard paratrooper to have done so.

Tom has served on the board of trustees for the Southwest Michigan Land Conservancy and the St. Joseph County (Michigan) Conservation District. He also serves as a lector and jail ministry leader for Immaculate Conception Catholic Church in Three Rivers, Michigan. Tom holds a master's degree in journalism from the Knight Center for Environmental Journalism at Michigan State University in East Lansing.